THE NEIGHBORS HAVE TWO FLAMINGOS.

© 2013 Brad Diller

All Rights reserved. No part of this book may be reproduced or transmitted in any form by any means, electronic or mechanical, including photocopying, recording, or by any information storage and retrieval system, without written permission from the Publisher.

Published by Willow Creek Press, Inc.
P.O. Box 147, Minocqua, Wisconsin 54548

Design: William Letcher
Printed in the United States

The Neighbors Have Two Flamingos.

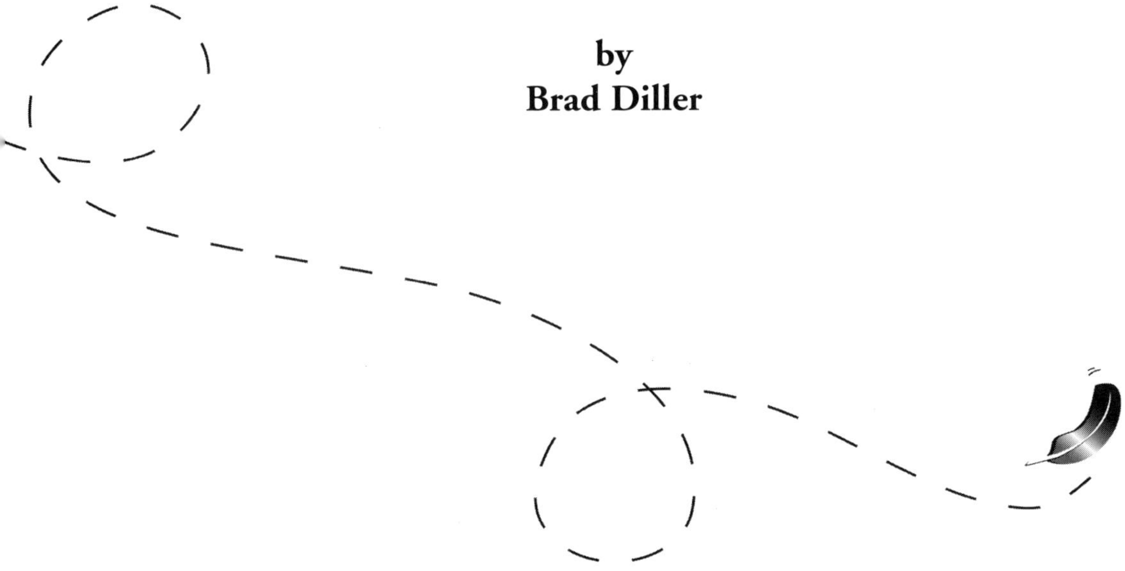

by
Brad Diller

WILLOW CREEK PRESS®

Dedicated to Lee, who believed in me, even when I stopped.

Acknowledgements:

The Neighbors Have Two Flamingos is the accumulation of ten years in cartooning and I am deeply indebted to so many people. If I've left anyone out, I apologize in advance.

Thanks to Dave Greenfield and the staff at the Charleston Daily Mail in Charleston, WV. for giving me a chance and publishing my cartoons. I'm forever grateful for your generosity.

To my business partners, Seth Sheck and Frank Himler; I can never thank you enough for allowing me the freedom to pursue my passion.

To Jay Perry and Larry Hughes who ~~shoved~~ pushed me through my self-imposed limitations. It was - and continues to be - an amazing ride.

To Sherri Del SolDato who loves cartoons and expressed that through my website.

To William Letcher for his vision and perseverance in designing this book. It's always a pleasure to work with you.

To the staff at Access Pass & Design. I'm deeply grateful to work with such an inspiring group of people every day.

A special thanks to my family – the funniest people I know.

To my wife Lee, who sees every variation of every joke and still laughs. I wouldn't be here without you.

Finally to my readers – there is no cartoon without you.

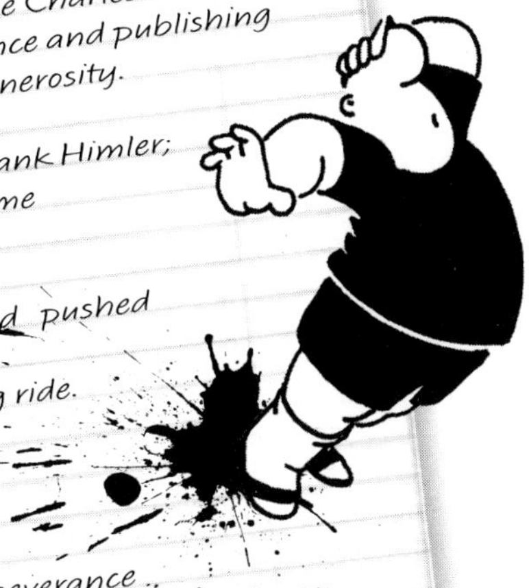

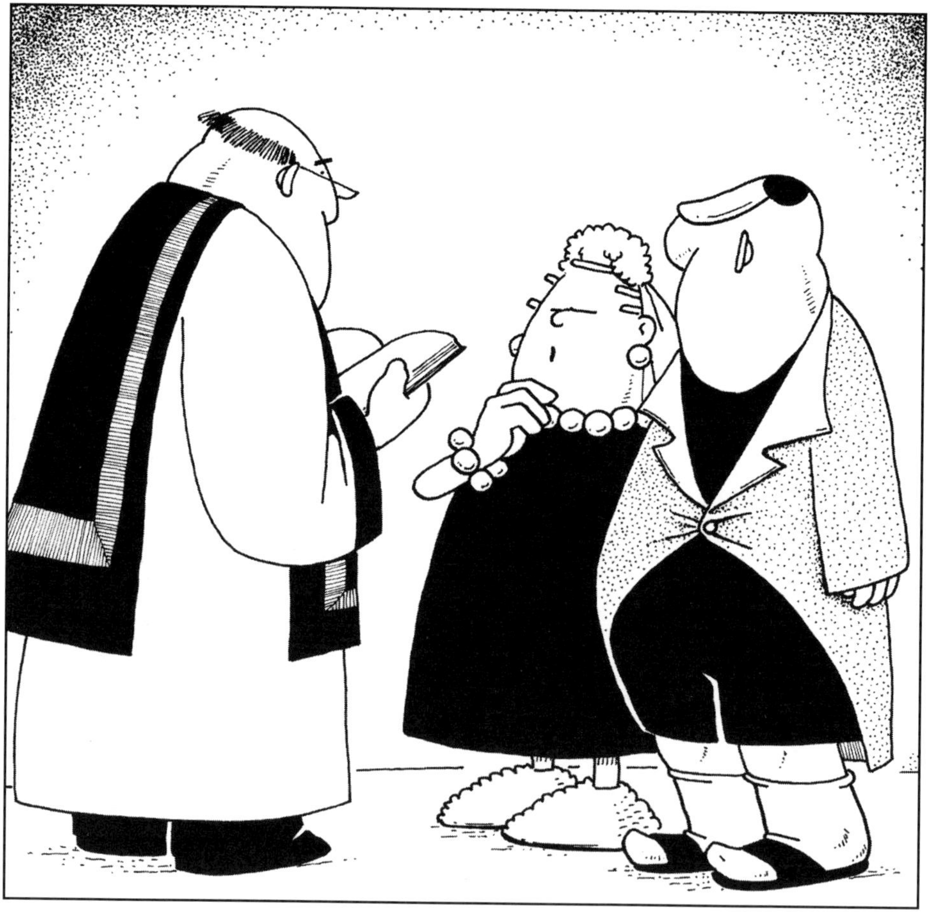

"Define 'worse.'"

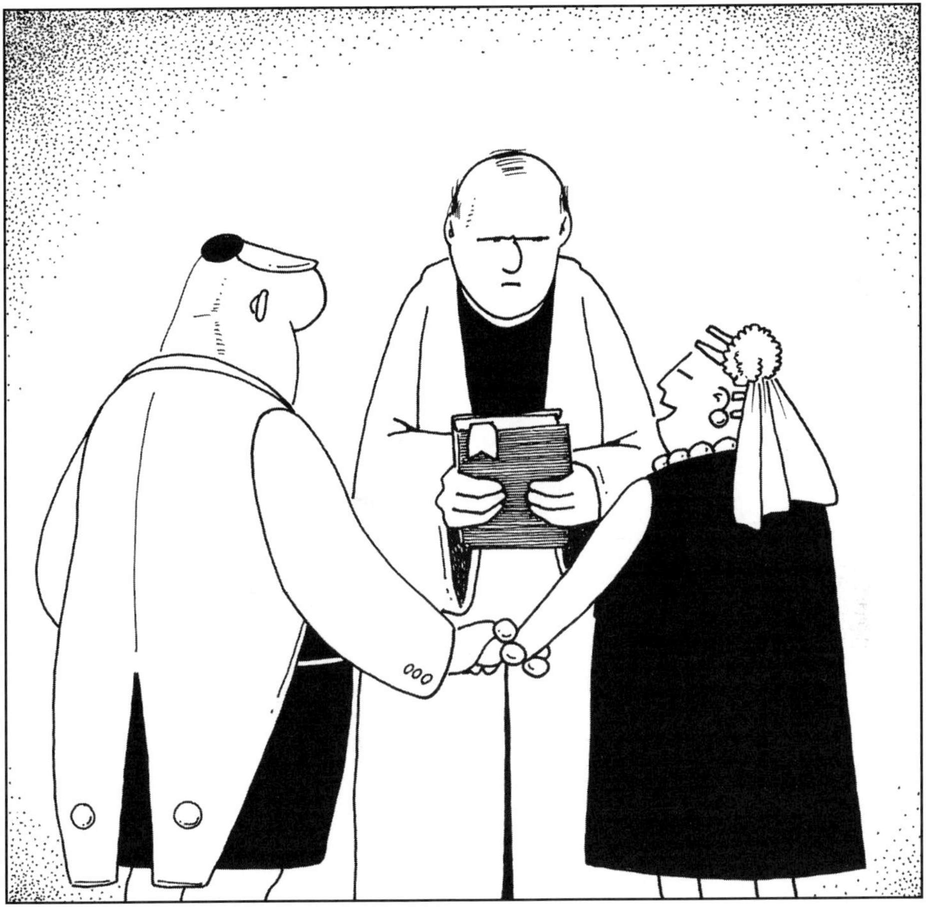

"He does."

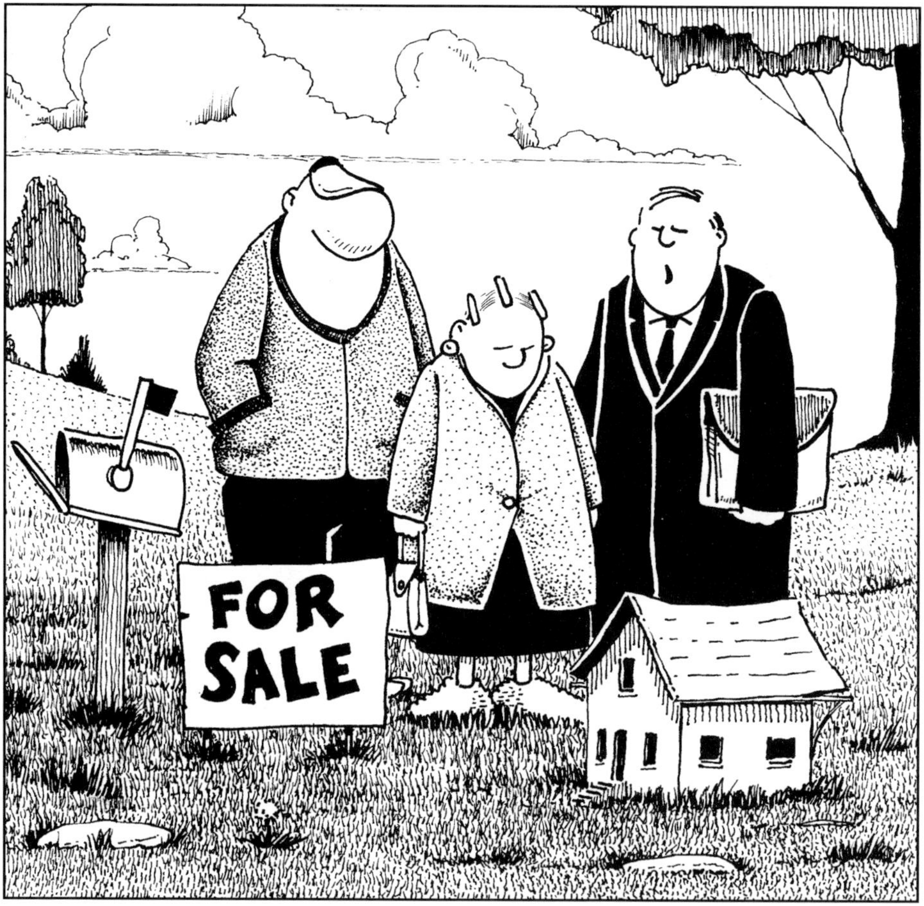
FOR
SALE

"Here's that little fixer-upper I told you about."

"Mom said to finish your nap. It's January."

"So, Winnie... When you write your name in the snow, is it number one or number two?"

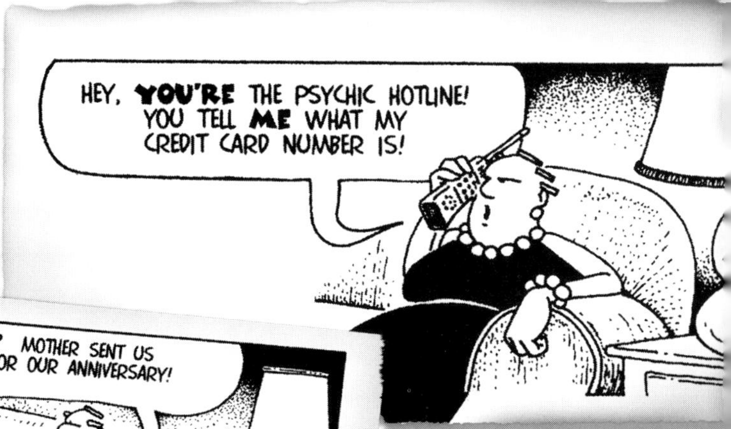
HEY, **YOU'RE** THE PSYCHIC HOTLINE! YOU TELL **ME** WHAT MY CREDIT CARD NUMBER IS!

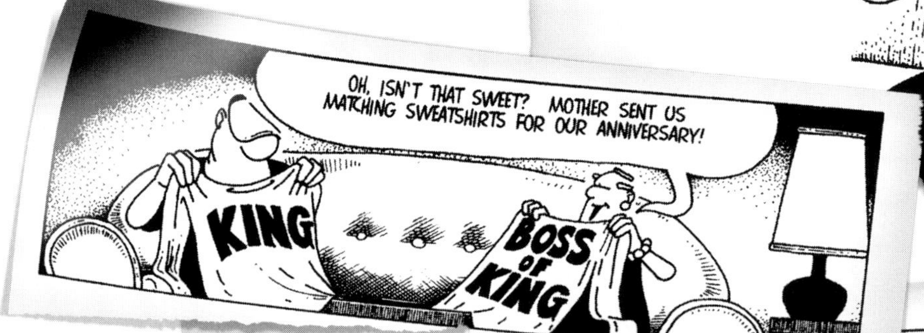
OH, ISN'T THAT SWEET? MOTHER SENT US MATCHING SWEATSHIRTS FOR OUR ANNIVERSARY!
KING
BOSS OF KING

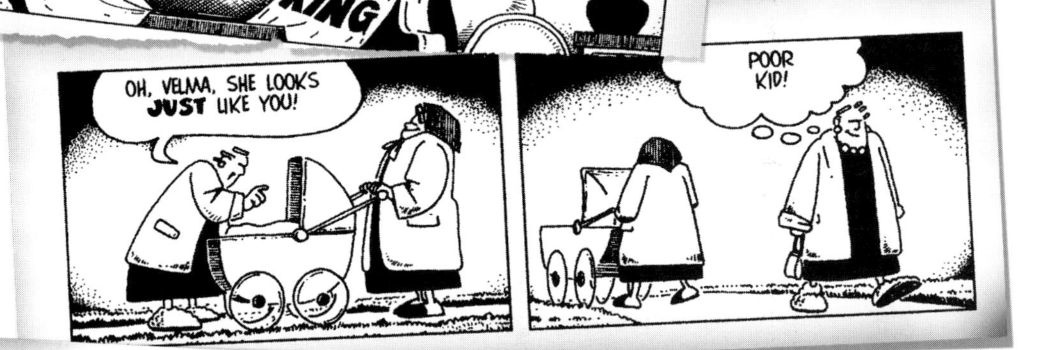
OH, VELMA, SHE LOOKS **JUST** LIKE YOU!
POOR KID!

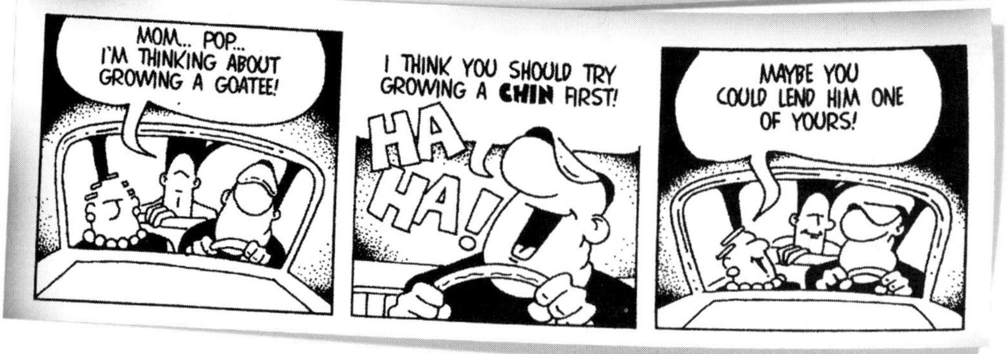
MOM... POP... I'M THINKING ABOUT GROWING A GOATEE!
I THINK YOU SHOULD TRY GROWING A **CHIN** FIRST!
HA HA HA!
MAYBE YOU COULD LEND HIM ONE OF YOURS!

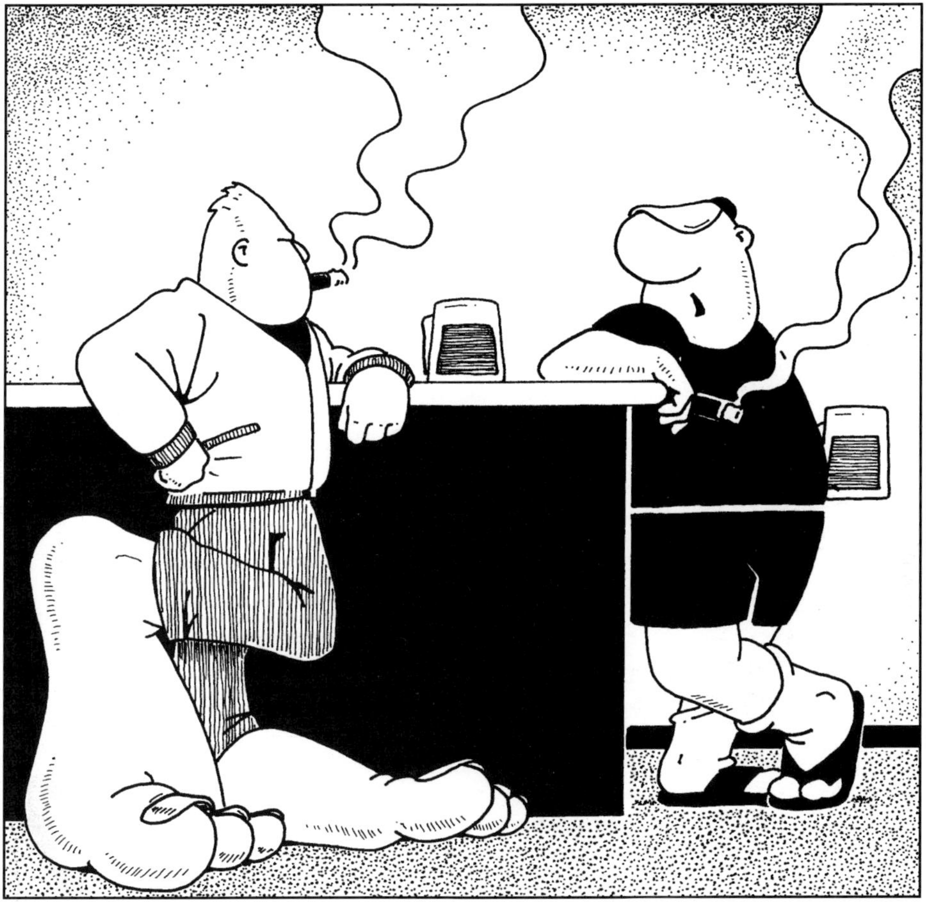

"Yeah, right! I suppose you have PROOF of this Bigfoot story of yours?"

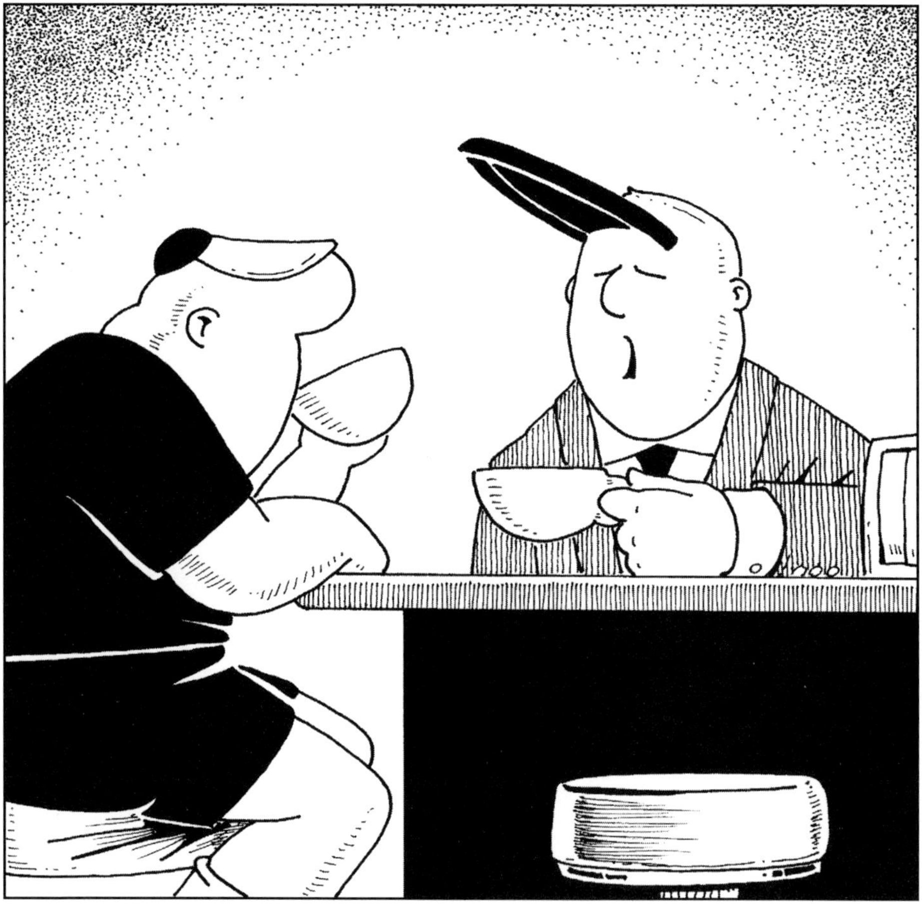

"And I sat there wondering... Why?
Why is that frisbee getting bigger?
Then it hit me."

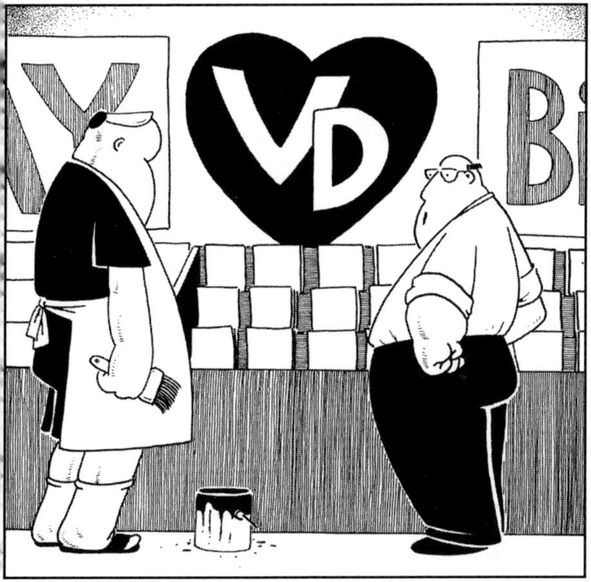
VD

"Do you think we should spell out 'Valentine's Day?'"

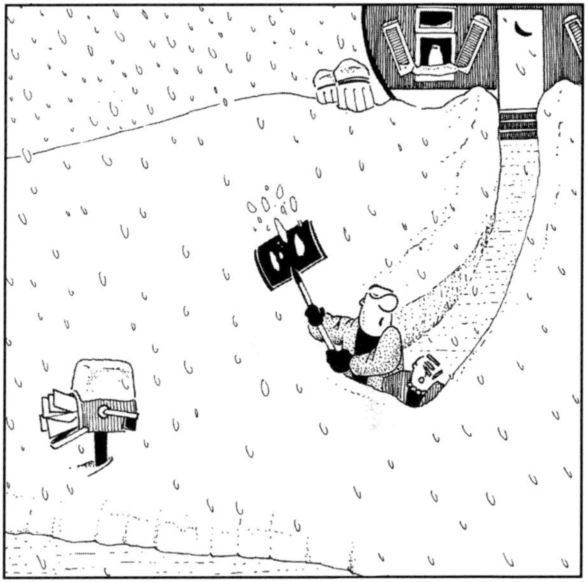

"There had better be a valentine in that mailbox!"

"'Umbrellas half off,' he said.
'What a bargain,' you said.
'What a crock,' I say."

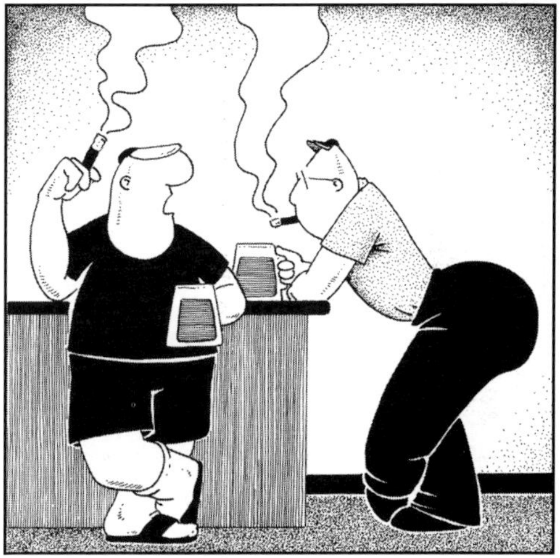

"Try day trading. I know lots of guys who lost their ass that way."

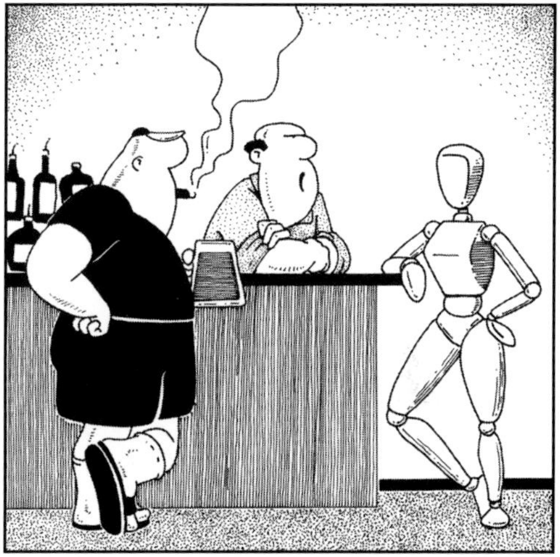

"I don't care if you are a model. You can't come in here naked."

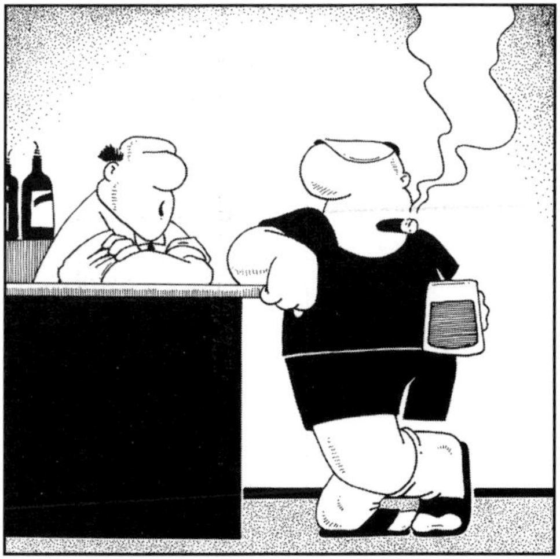

"Bud, let me give you some advice. It's free and I never use it."

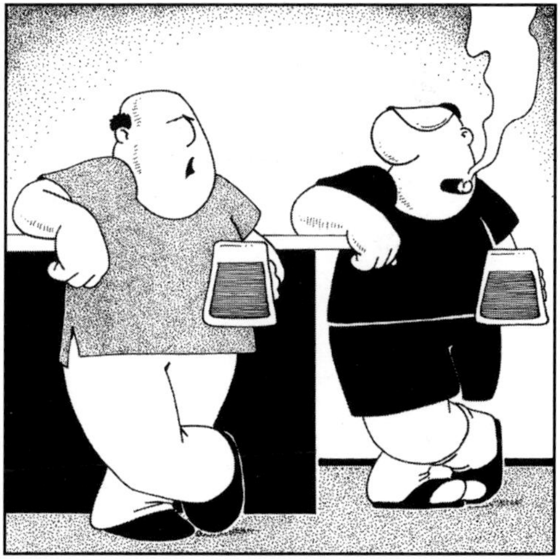

"I tell ya, Bud, I had it all... The wife... kids... the truck... a doublewide... a mullet..."

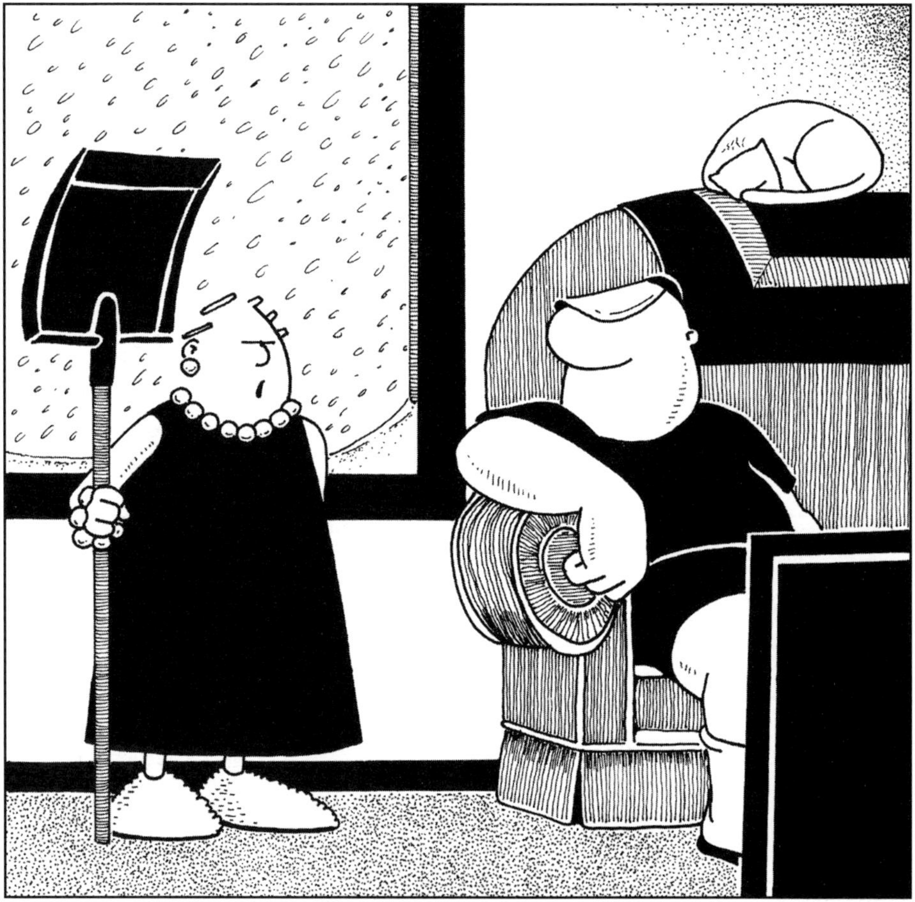

"How about shoveling the global warming off the driveway?"

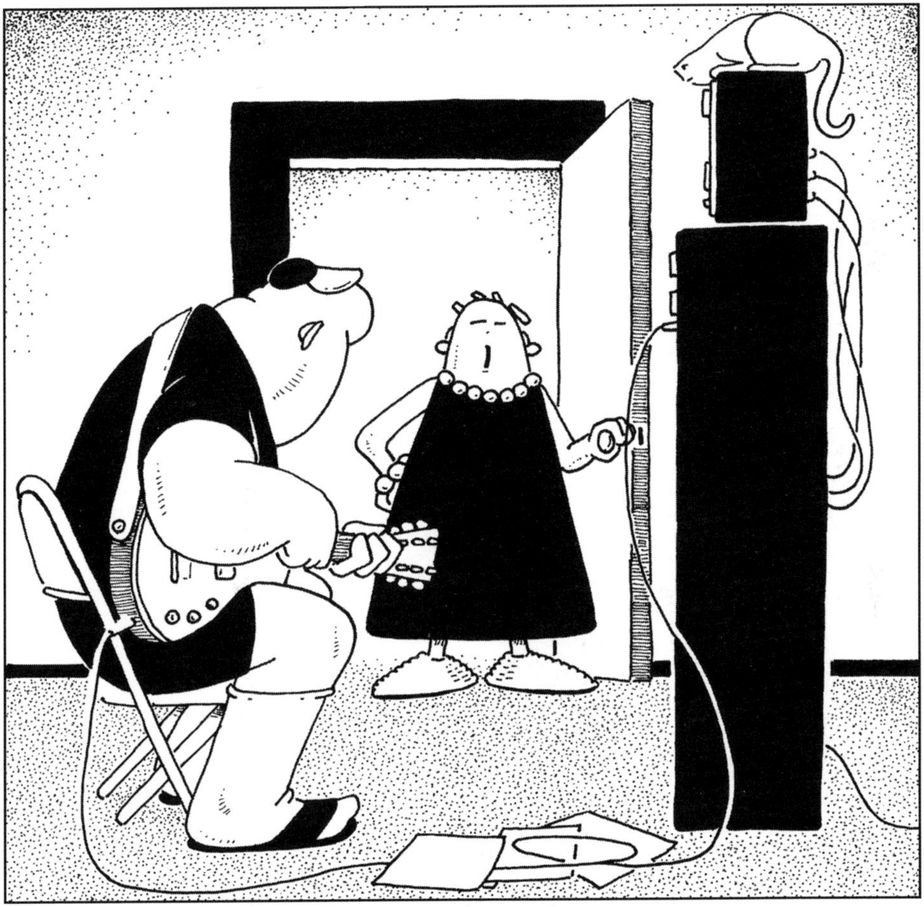

"If you're taking requests,
I'd love to hear 'The Sounds of Silence.'"

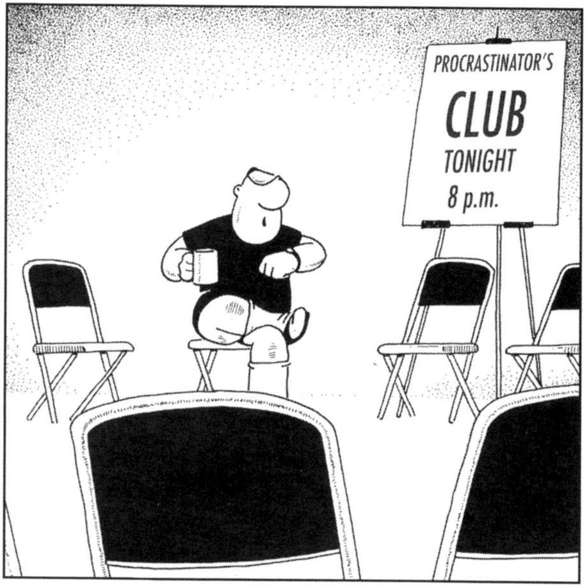
PROCRASTINATOR'S
CLUB
TONIGHT
8 p.m.

"Well... It's quarter after eight.
I guess I could get started..."

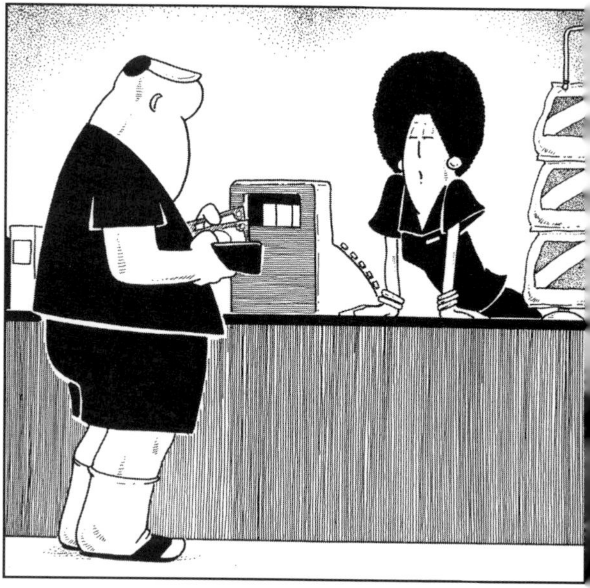

"I'm a cashier.
Of course I'm after your money."

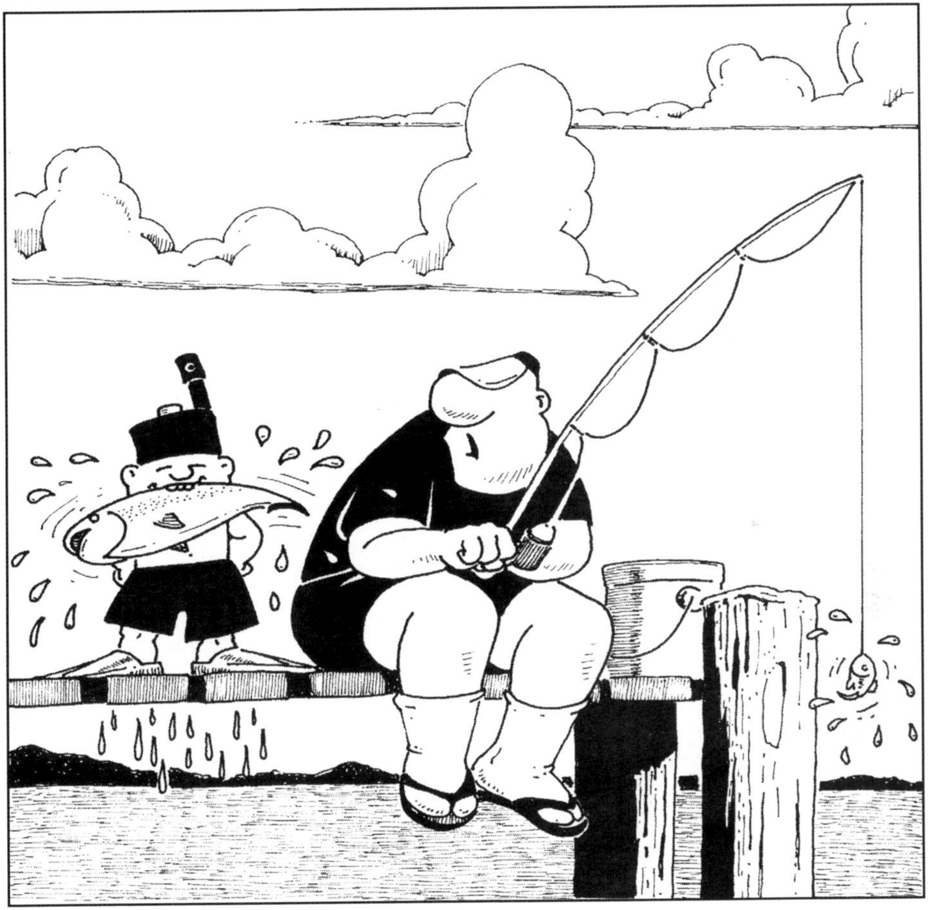

"Show off."

"Do autopsies hurt?"

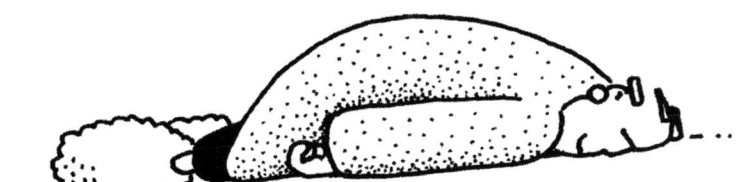

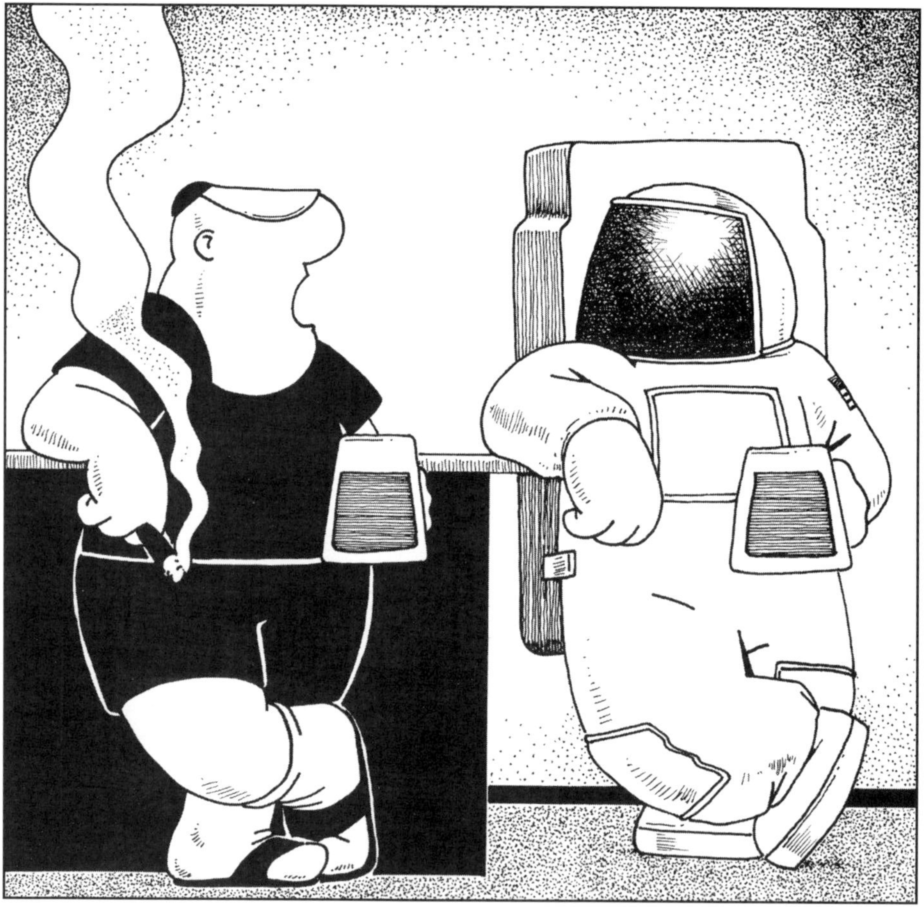

"So... Is the sky the limit?"

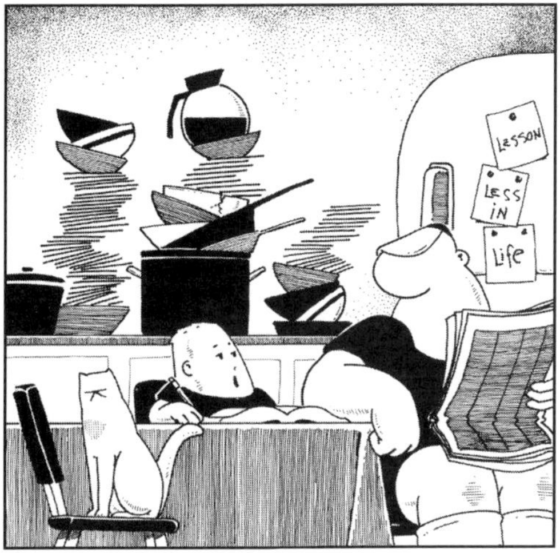
LESSON
LESS IN
Life

"If I'm never going to amount to anything, why do I have to do homework?"

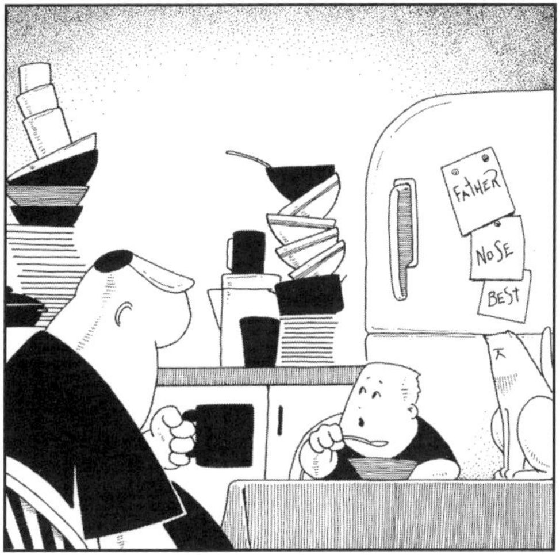
FATHER
NOSE
BEST

"Pop, when I grow up, will I be as ugly as you?"

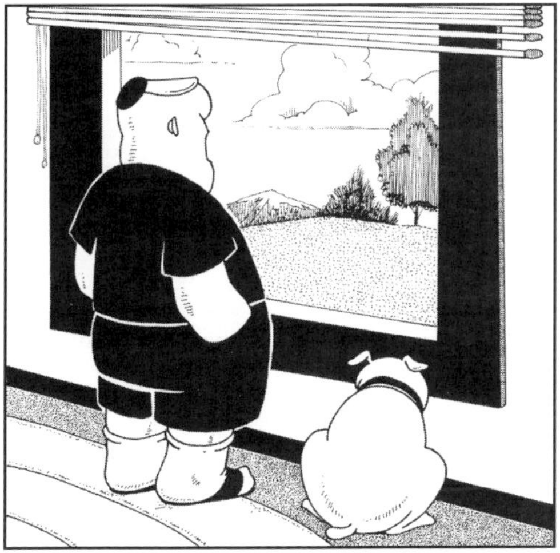

"Looks like Spring is here. I guess you and I should start using the bathroom outside again."

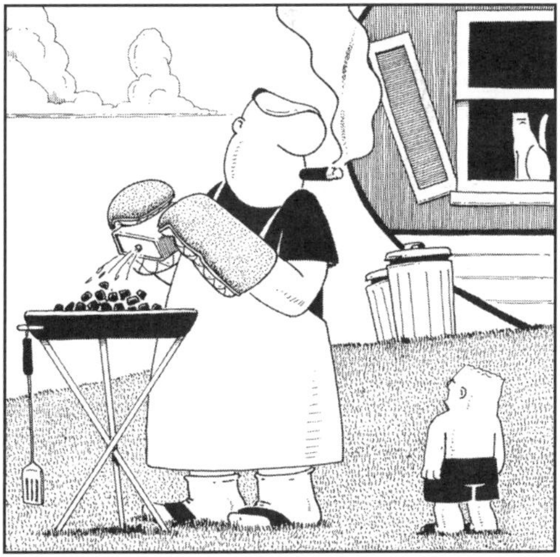

"Pop, could you hurry up and light the grill? Mom says it isn't officially summer until you blow your eyebrows off."

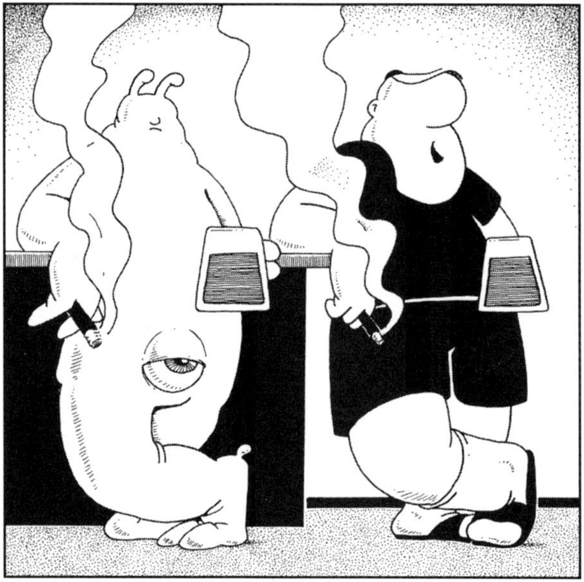

"Don't take it personally. A lot of cultures here on Earth consider it rude to look someone in the eye."

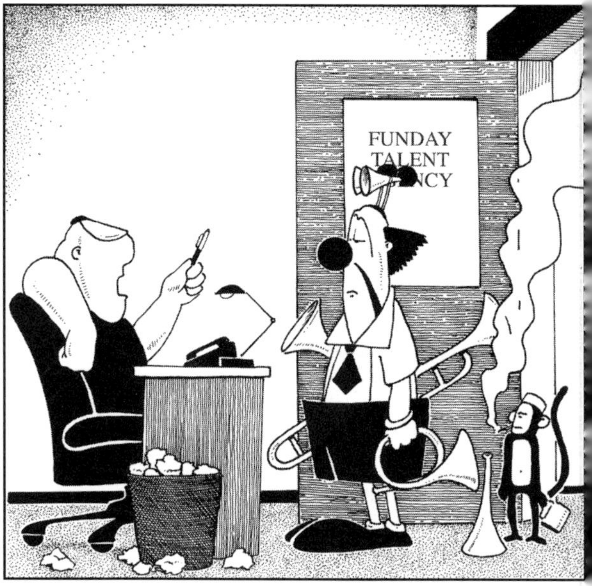
FUNDAY

"Love the act. But, I'm not sure how well the name 'Horny the Clown and his Smoking Monkey' is going to play with the kid's birthday crowd."

"And what does your husband do for the I.R.S.?"

"Have a seat. It's time for your annual review."

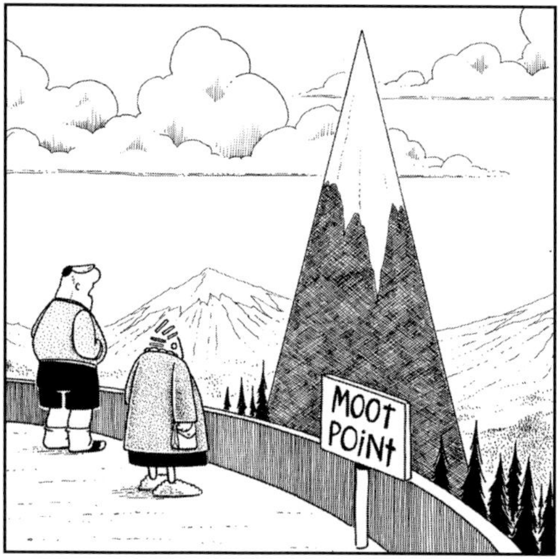
MOOT
POINT

"It's just like I imagined."

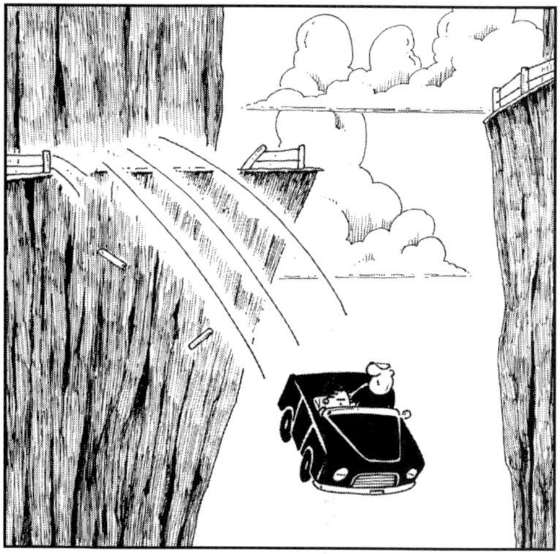

"At least we're making good time."

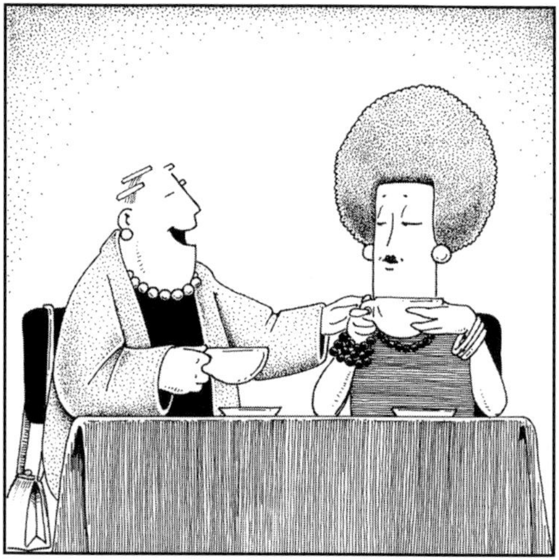

"When you find 'Mr. Right,' dear, make sure his first name isn't 'Always.'"

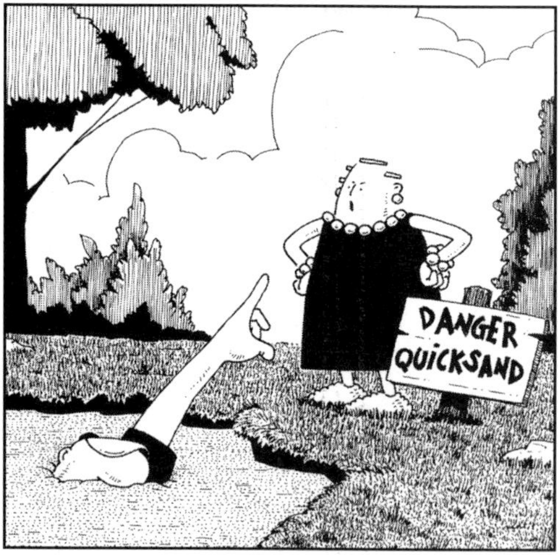
DANGER
QUICKSAND

"After ten years of marriage, do you really expect me to pull your finger?"

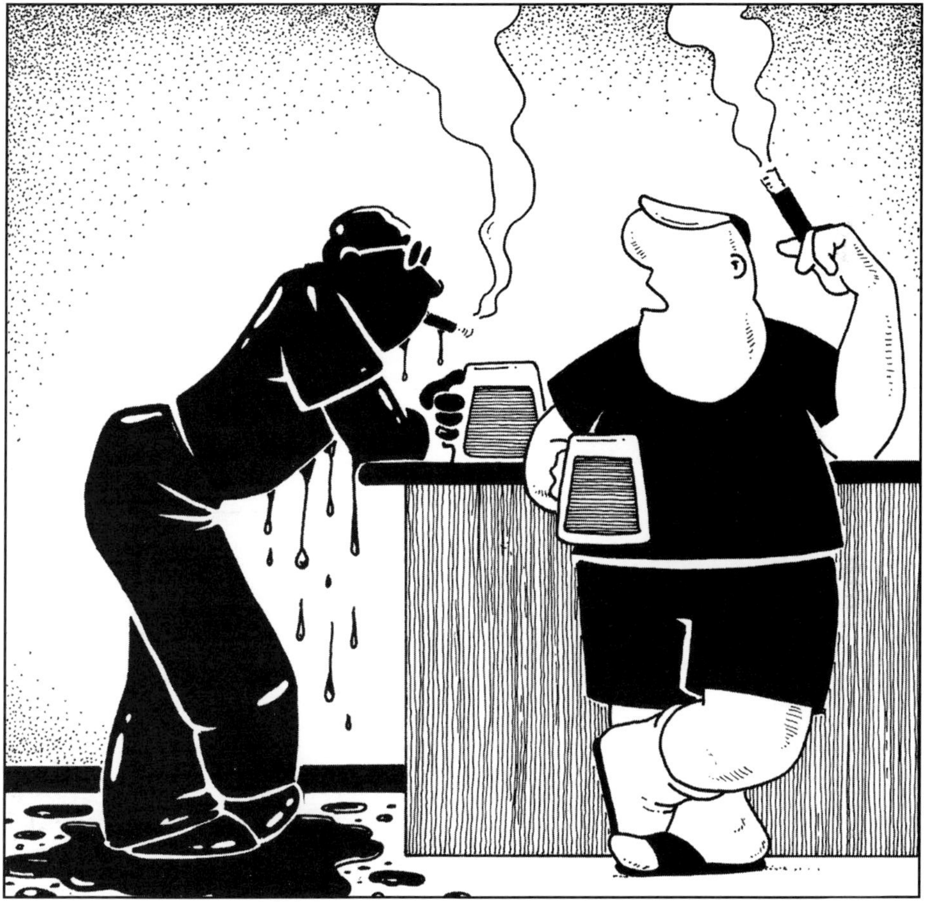

"How was the beach?"

"Coach, we've been together for three seasons now, and we were wondering... What's it feel like to win?"

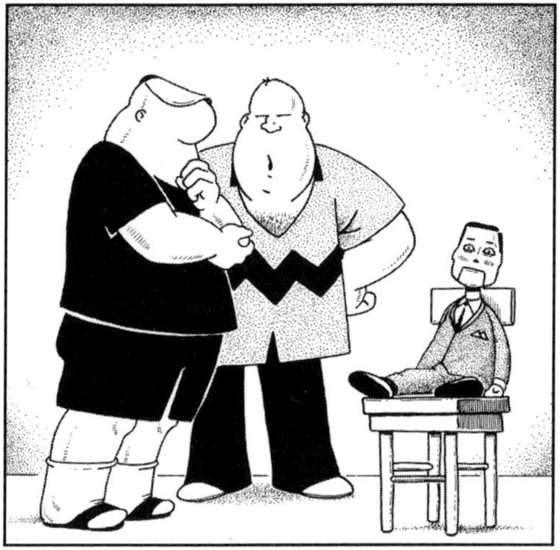

"Trust me, you do NOT want to know what I had to do to get him to talk."

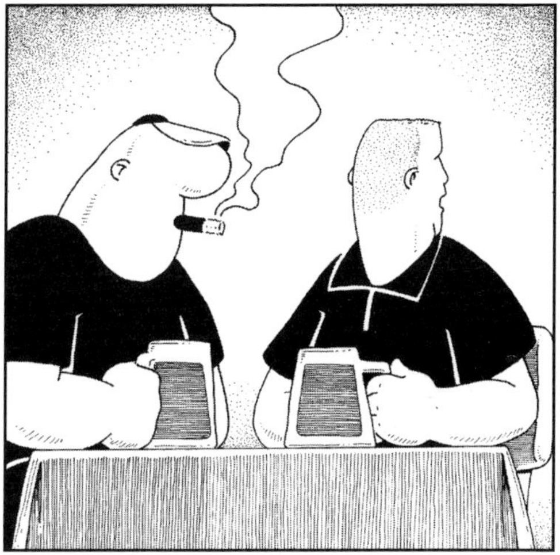

"Call me a pessimist, but I can't seem to look forward to anything."

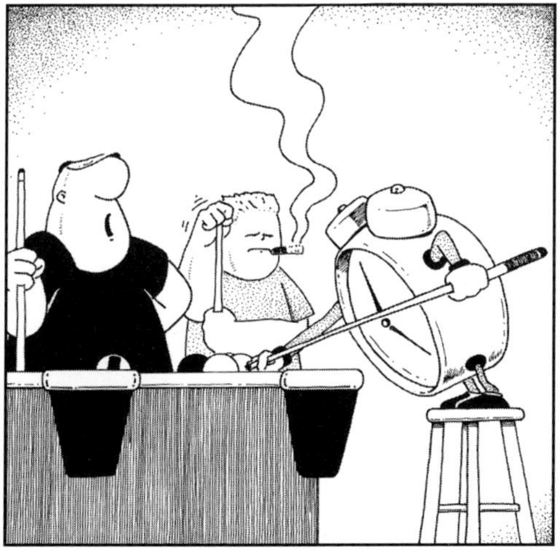

"I've always wondered where the time goes."

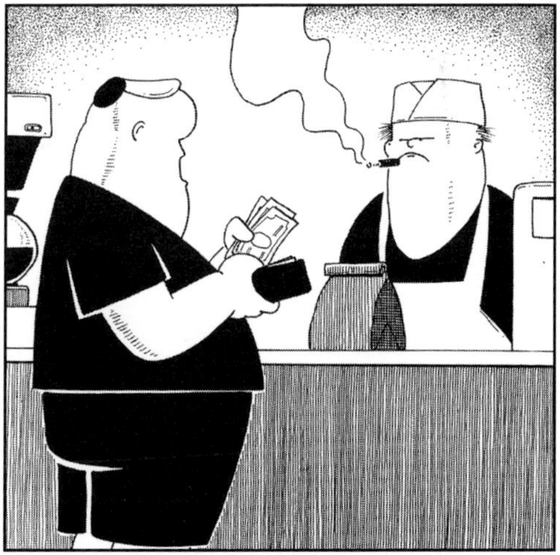

"Since you're charging me through the nose, is it okay if I pay you with mucus?"

"Checking to see if you're still ugly?"

"Let me rephrase that. Let's shoot the breeze."

"It's Mother's Day this Sunday. Want to go to Hooters?"

"As long as you're in there, I'll take a Dorito."

"The... Uh... The babysitter used laundry soap in the dishwasher... and... and... it got rabies! So, I had to tie her up!"

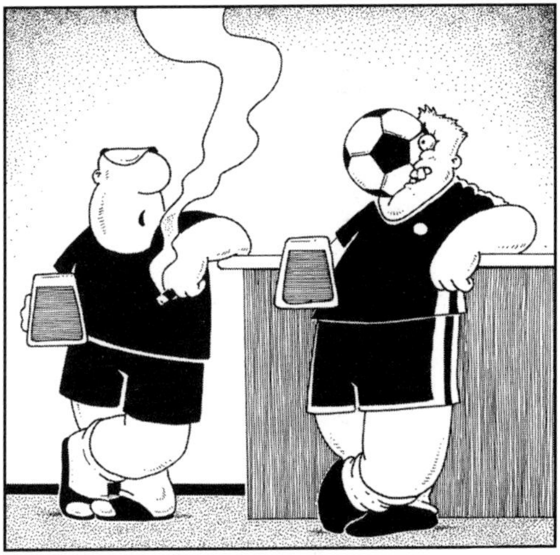

"Look at the bright side. You saved the game and chicks dig scars."

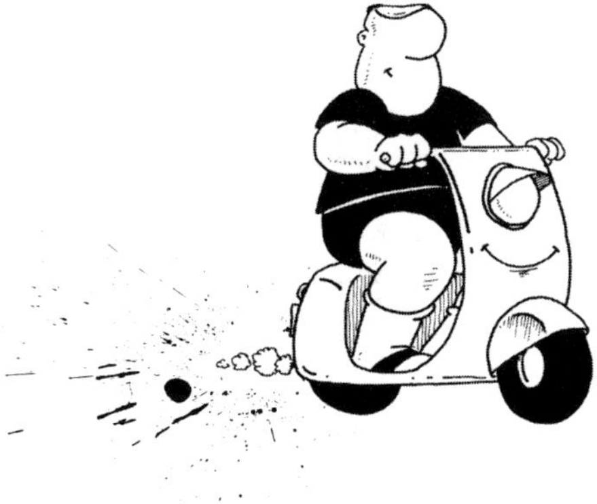

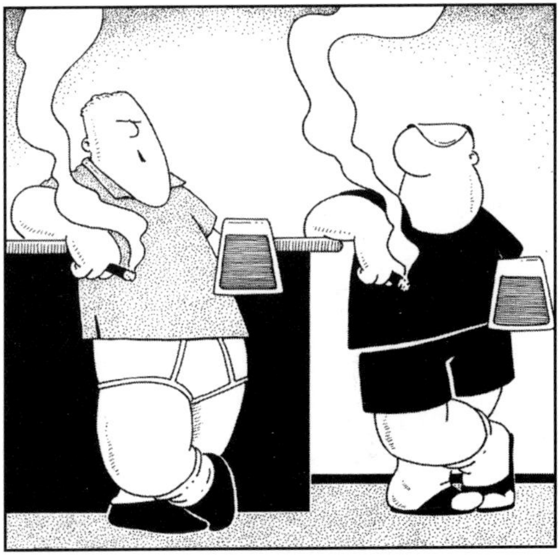

"My therapist said to follow my dreams and I keep having one where I'm in public in my underwear."

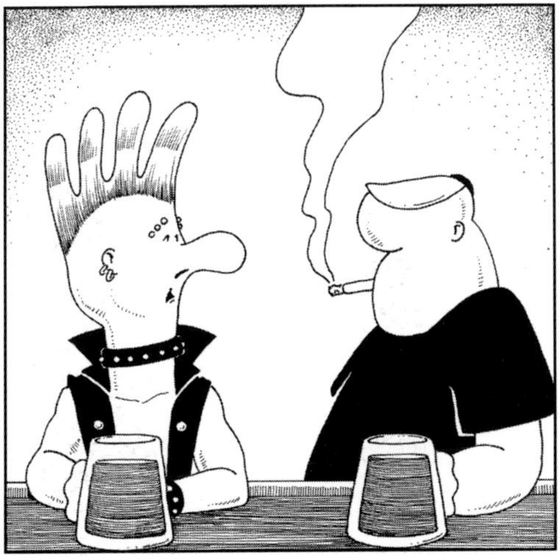

"Yeah, the mohawk's cool, but I'm getting a little tired of people high-fiving my face."

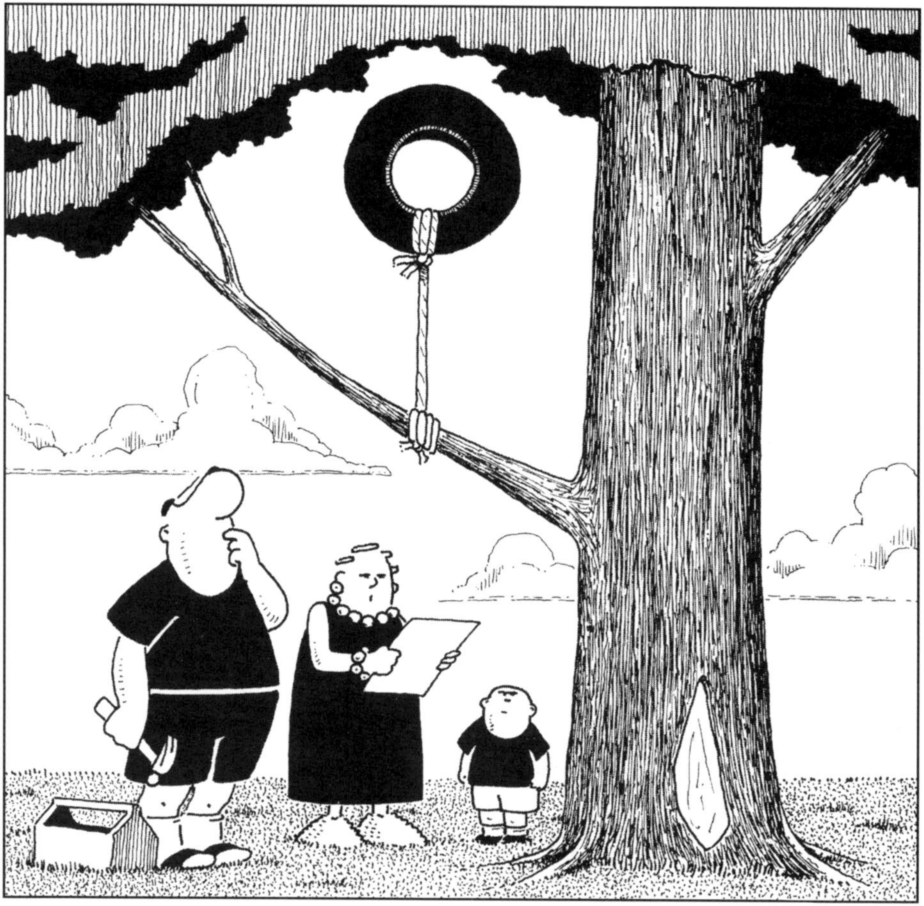

"Here's your problem.
You had the instructions upside down."

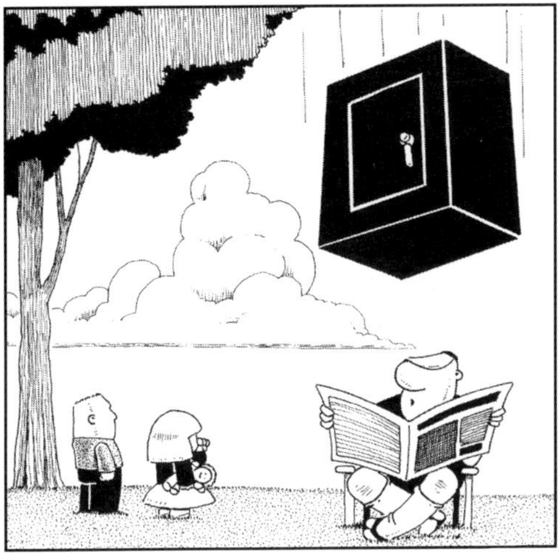

"An allowance? What... Do you kids think money just falls out of the sky?"

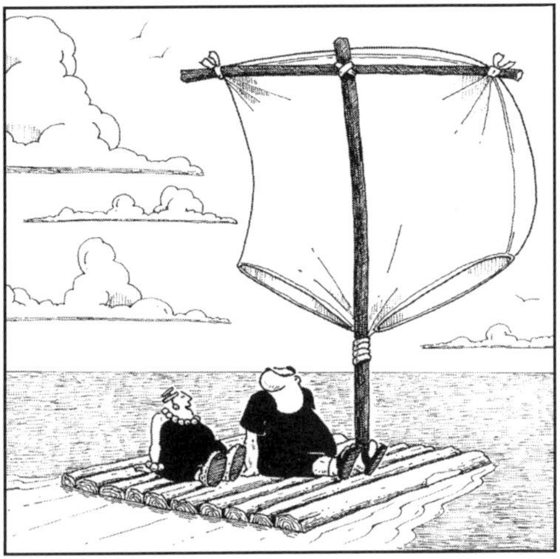

"NOW are you sorry I wore my granny panties on our little getaway cruise?"

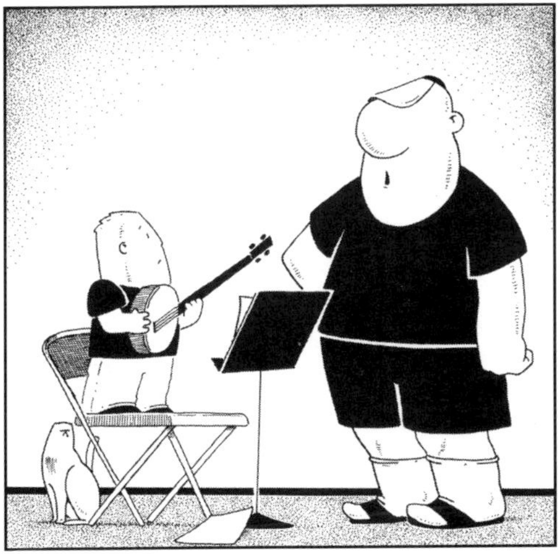

"Certainly, a law degree is a worthwhile endeavor, son, but you need something to fall back on. Now, practice your banjo."

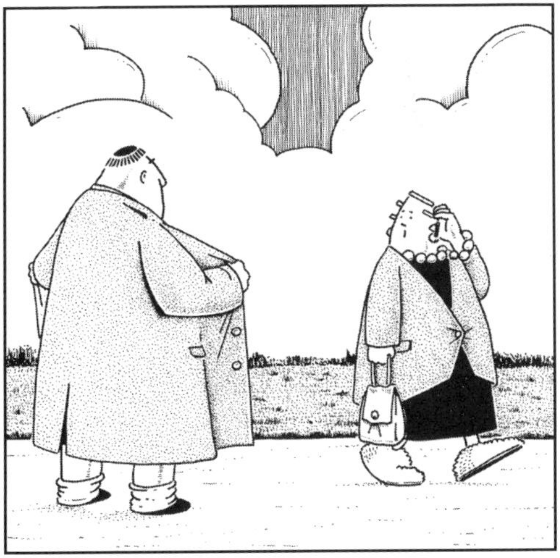

"Oh! While I'm thinking about it, sweetheart, will you pick up some Kibbles 'N' Bits on your way home?"

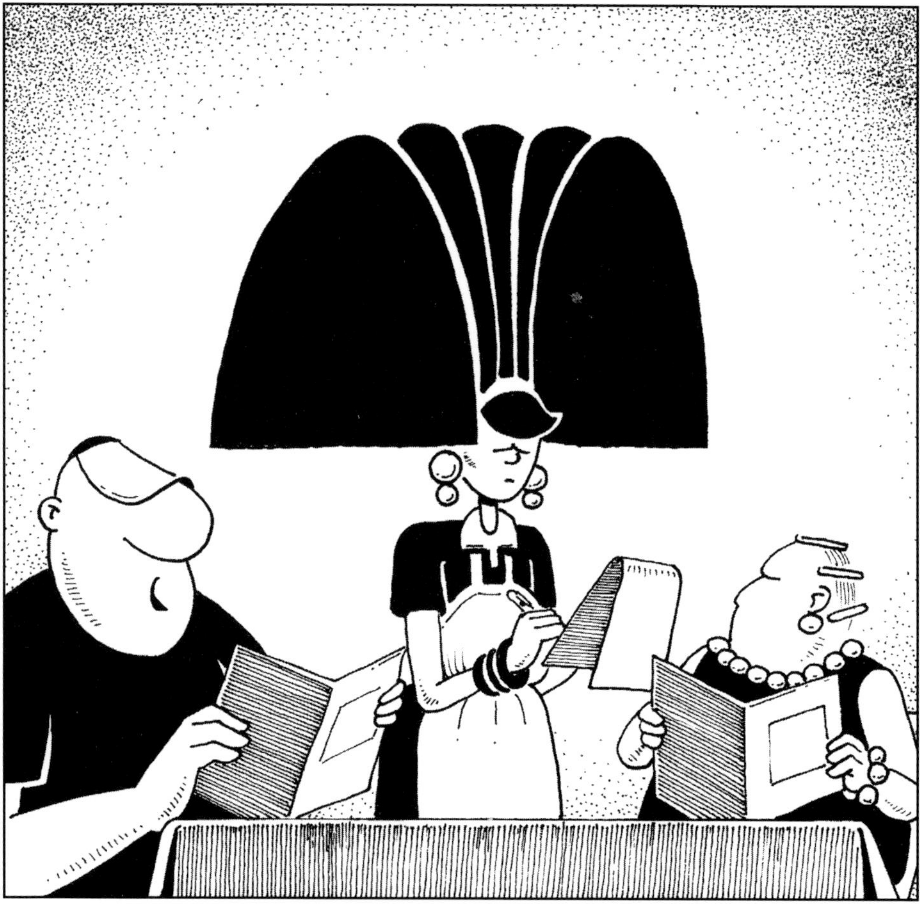

"Strange... I suddenly have a craving for bundt cake."

"Here's to Thursday!
The next best thing to Friday!"

"Thanks for the dissertation on the wages of sin, Padre, but I'd really like to hear more about your vows of silence."

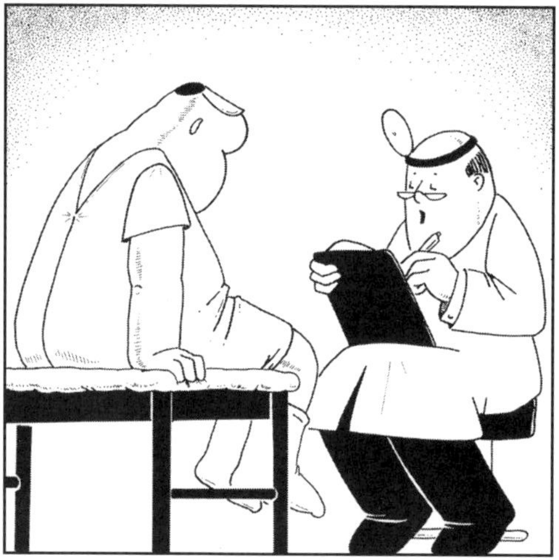

"You appear to be in perfect health, but keep in mind, I'm a pathologist."

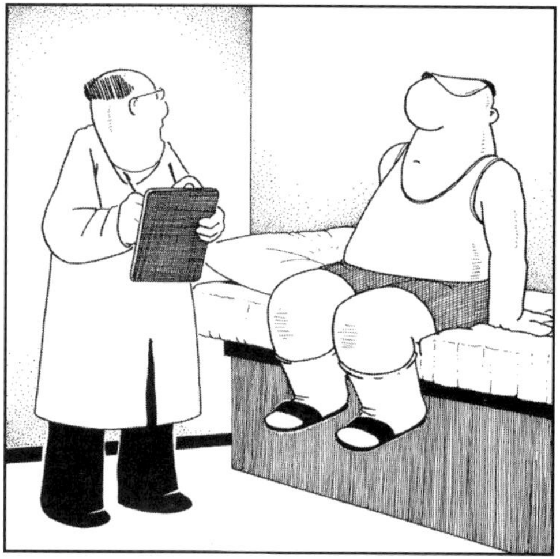

"You're in luck! You have twenty minutes to live and your health care covers that."

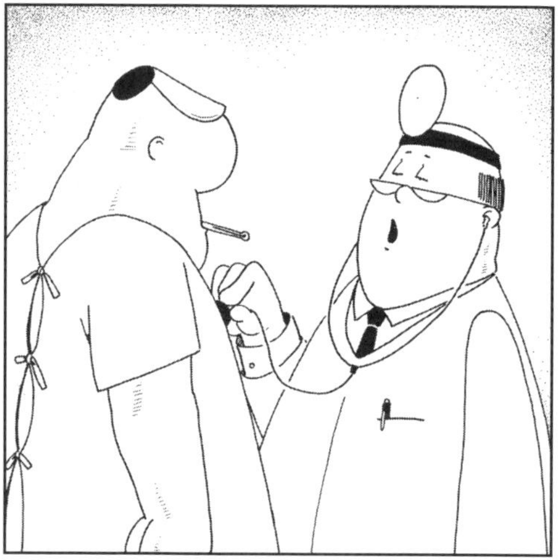

"My bill should be just the prescription for your incurable optimism."

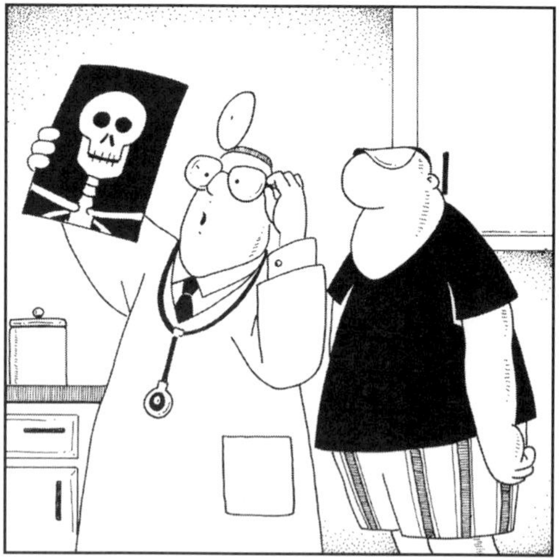

"Interesting... I thought ugly to the bone was just a saying."

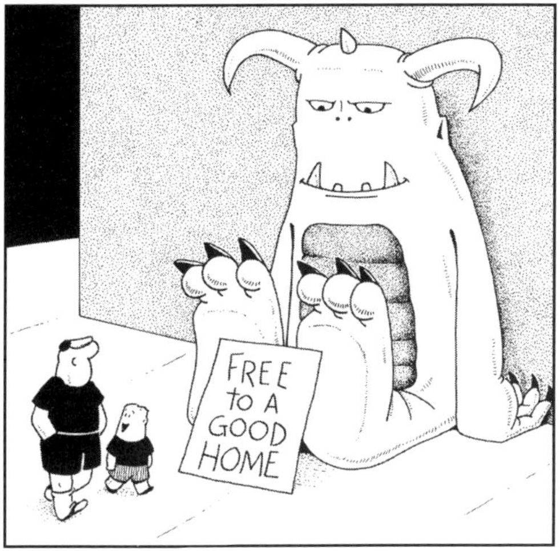
FREE
to A
GOOD
HOME
"Can we keep him?"

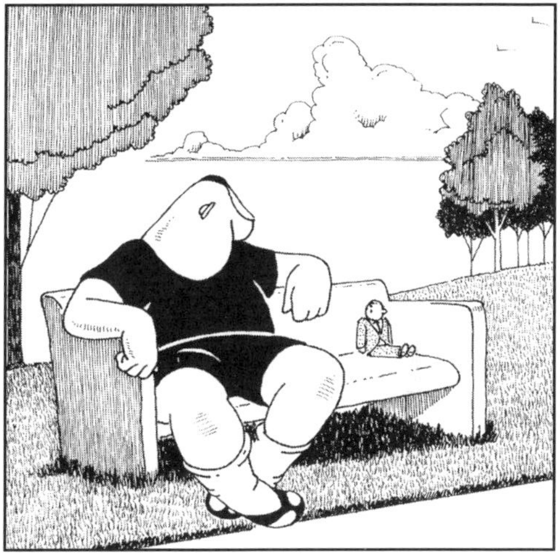
"I tend to sweat the small stuff."

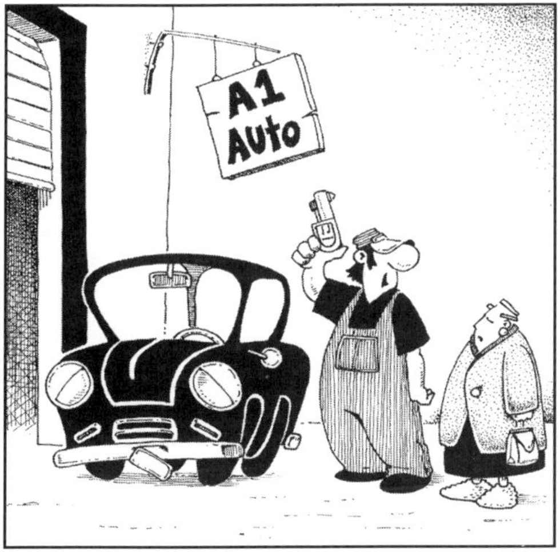
A1
AUTO
"Better turn your head.
This is not for the squeamish."

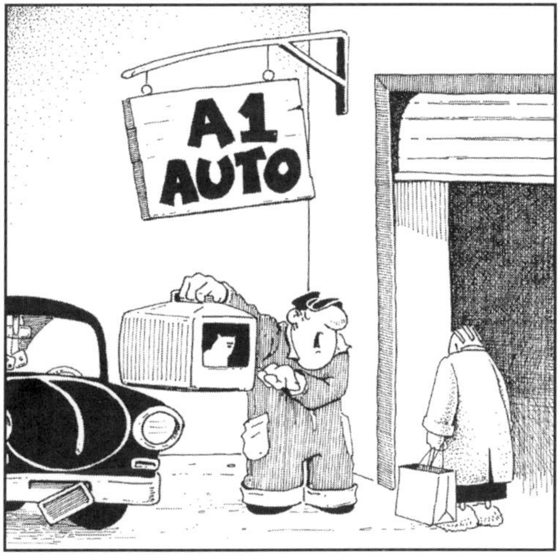
A1
AUTO
"I found the howling noise...
Your cat was under the seat.
That'll be $3500."

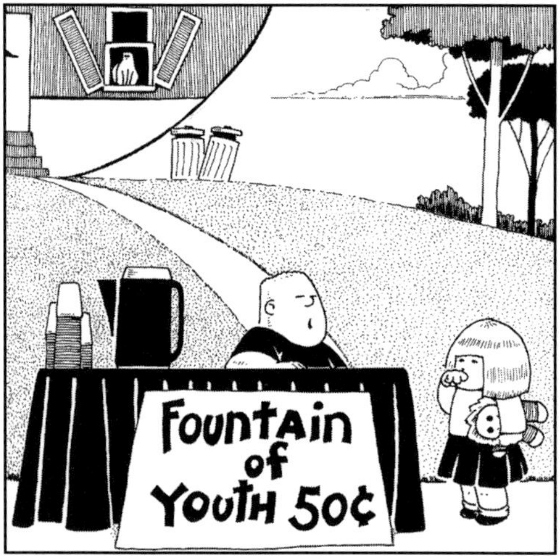
Fountain of Youth 50¢

"Now, remember, Peaches.
If anyone asks, you're my grandmother."

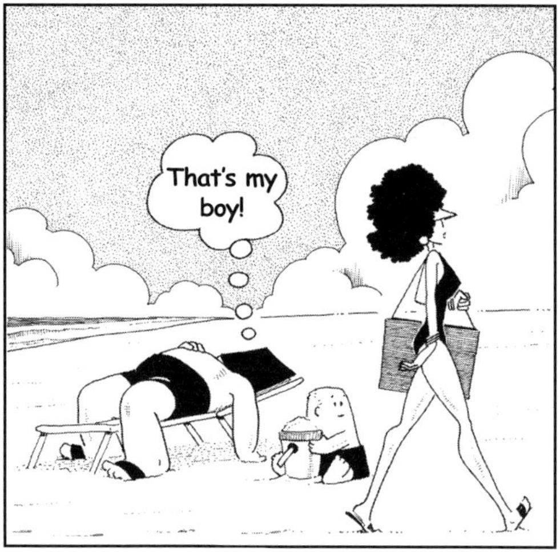
That's my boy!

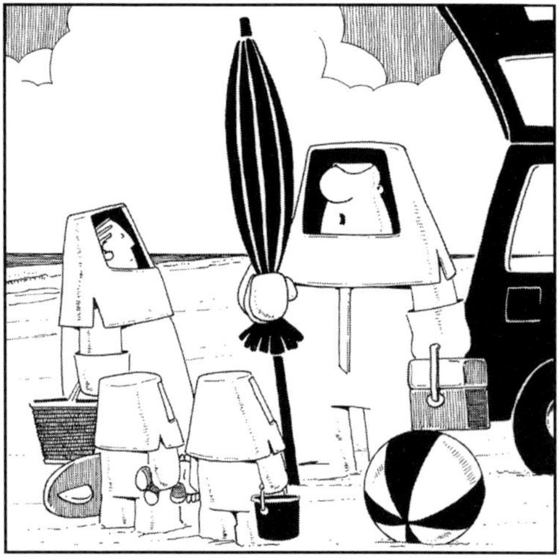

"Am I getting old, or is the beach not as much fun as it used to be?"

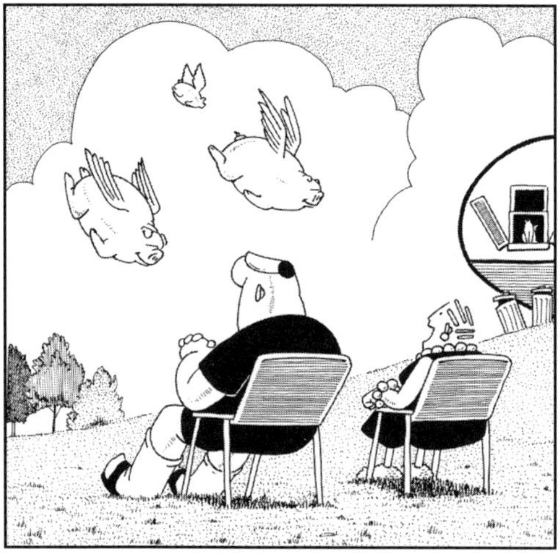

"Oh, look! Now the kids will clean their rooms, the check will be in the mail, and you'll take out the trash without asking."

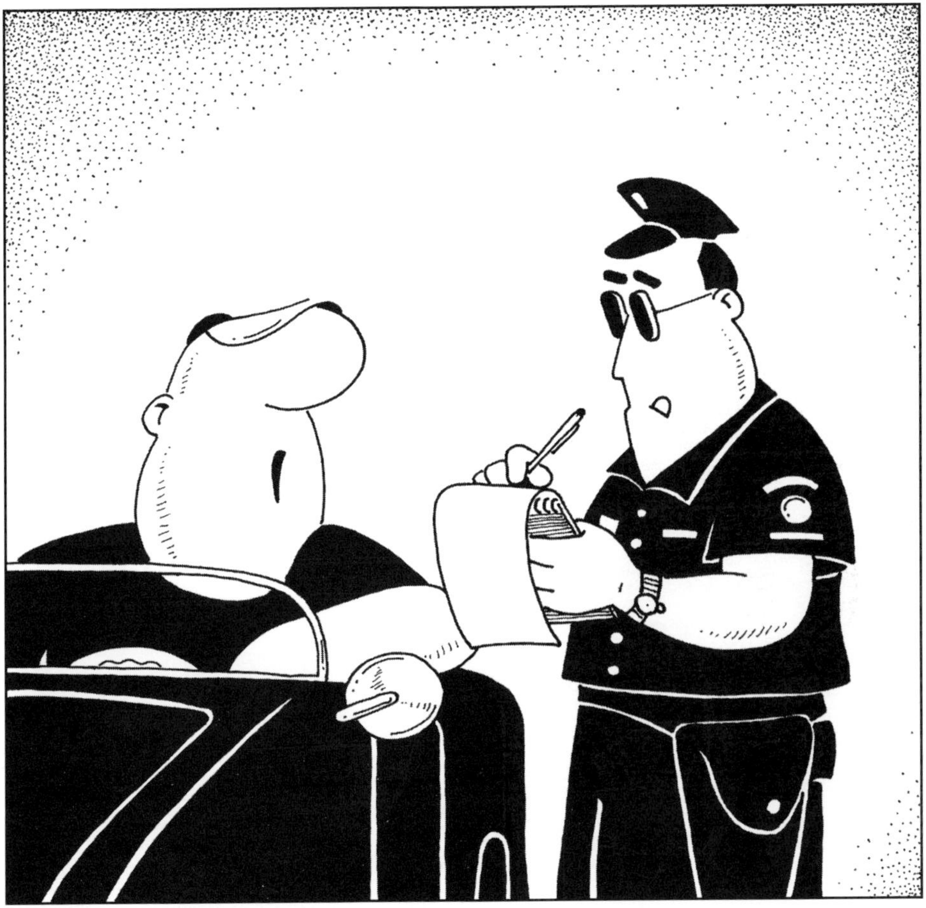

"You try holding a sandwich, a Big Gulp, and driving a manual transmission while texting, and tell me you don't have trouble maintaining lanes."

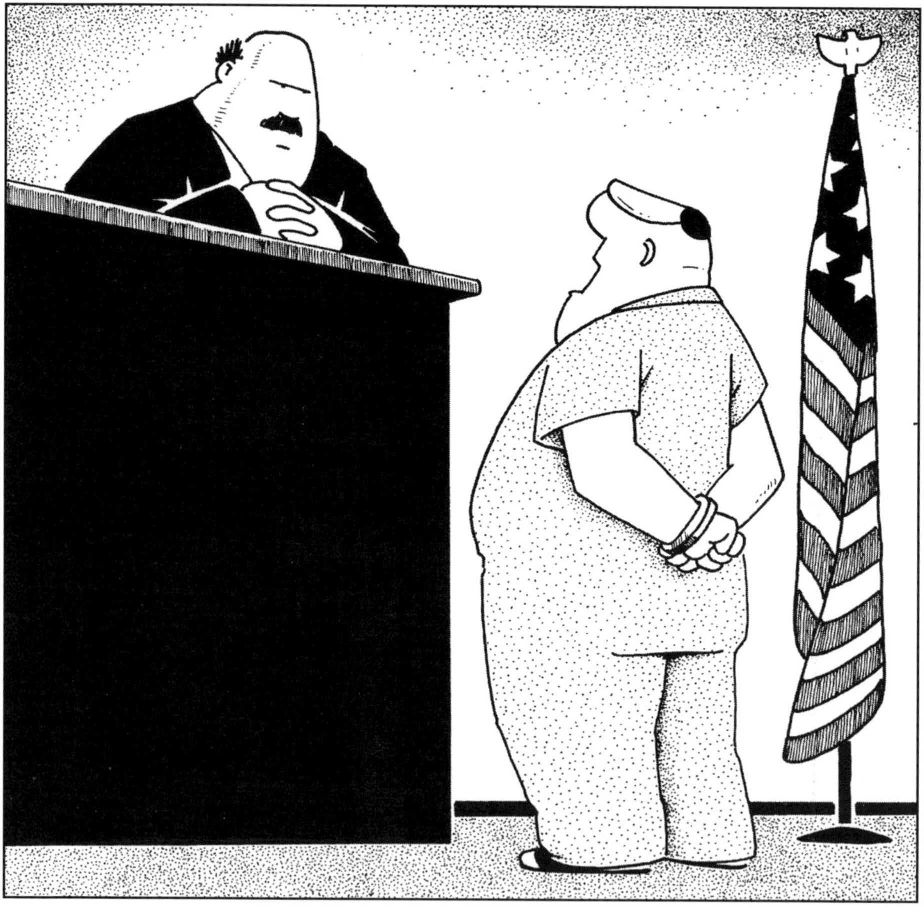

"Let me get this straight... I get three meals a day, healthcare, a warm place to sleep, and all I have to do is plead guilty?"

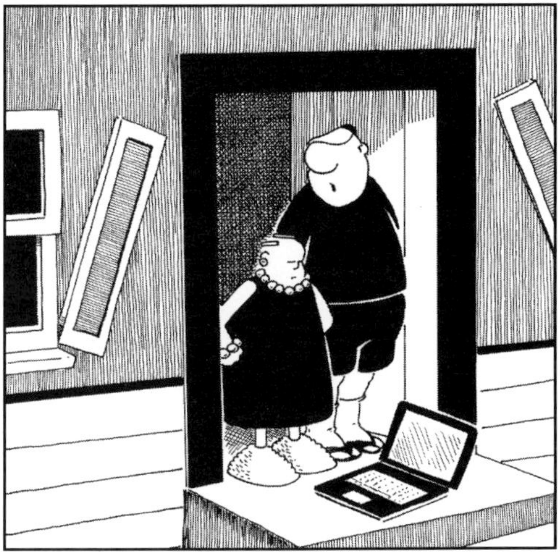

"If that's the newspaper, what are we going to use to housebreak the dog?"

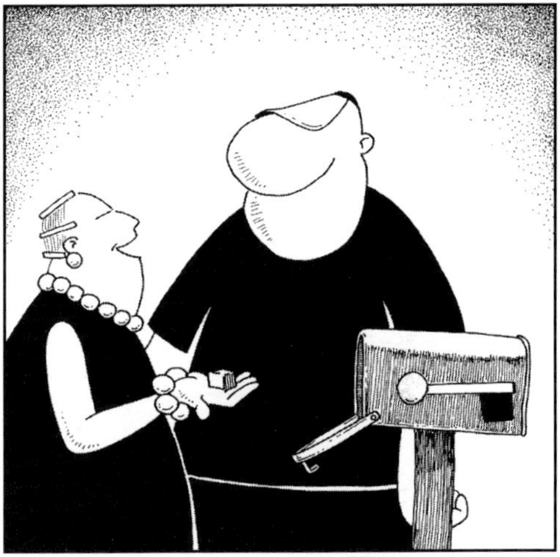

"Looks like our economic stimulus package finally arrived."

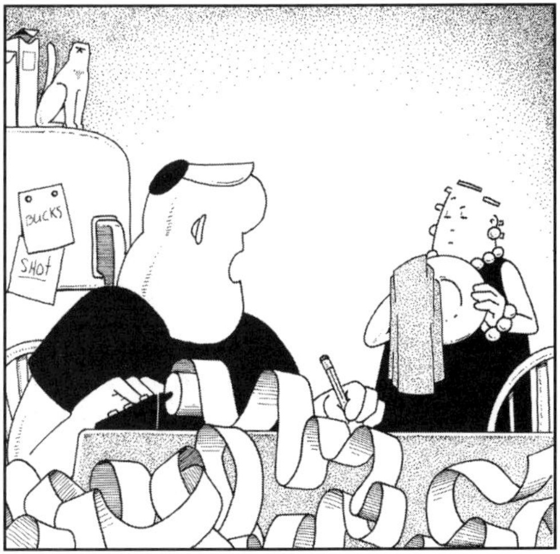
BUCKS
SHOT

"Well, we were going for broke and I think I can safely say, we've accomplished our goal."

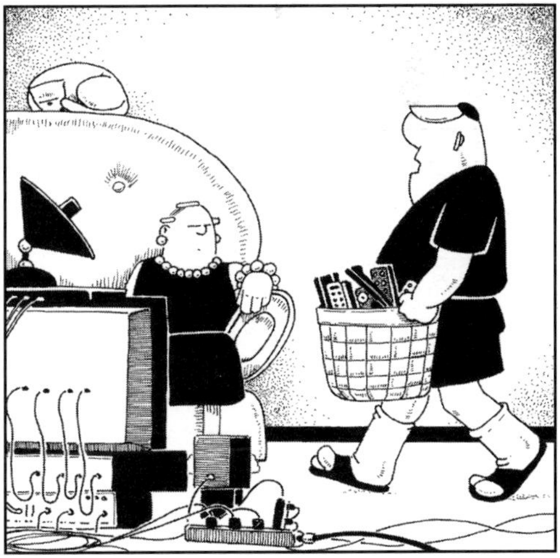

"I THINK this is all the remote controls. Let's watch a movie."

"It's karma."

"Look at the bright side, sweetheart, we're set for life."

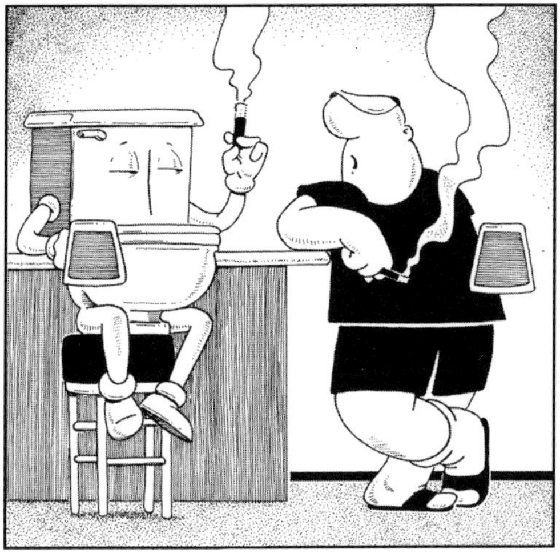

"Seriously, do you eat with that mouth?"

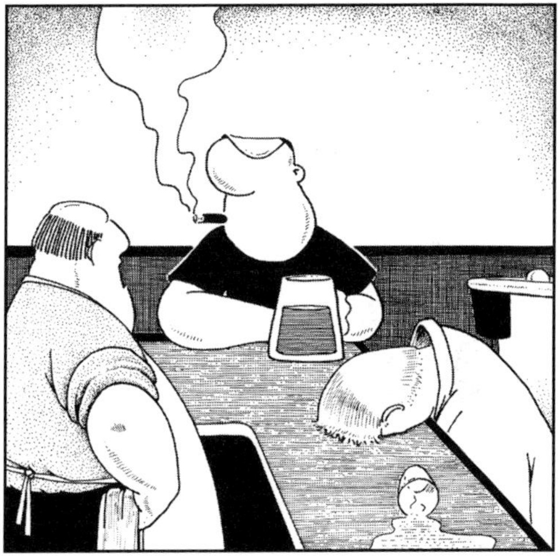

"His doctor said his liver was bad, so he came in here to teach it a lesson."

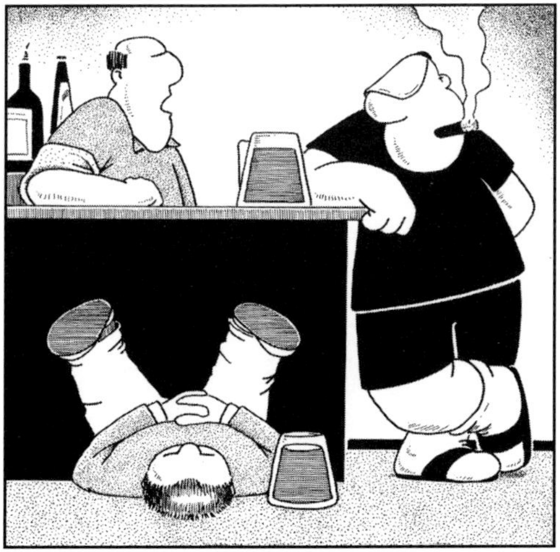

"He's been having his ups and downs. Today appears to be a down."

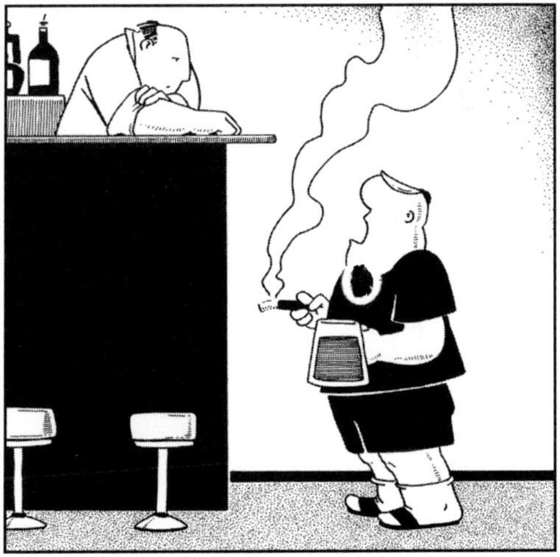

"I know you're trying for a better clientele, Scotty, but I think you set the bar too high."

"It appears you broke a wisdom tooth when you bit off more than you could chew."

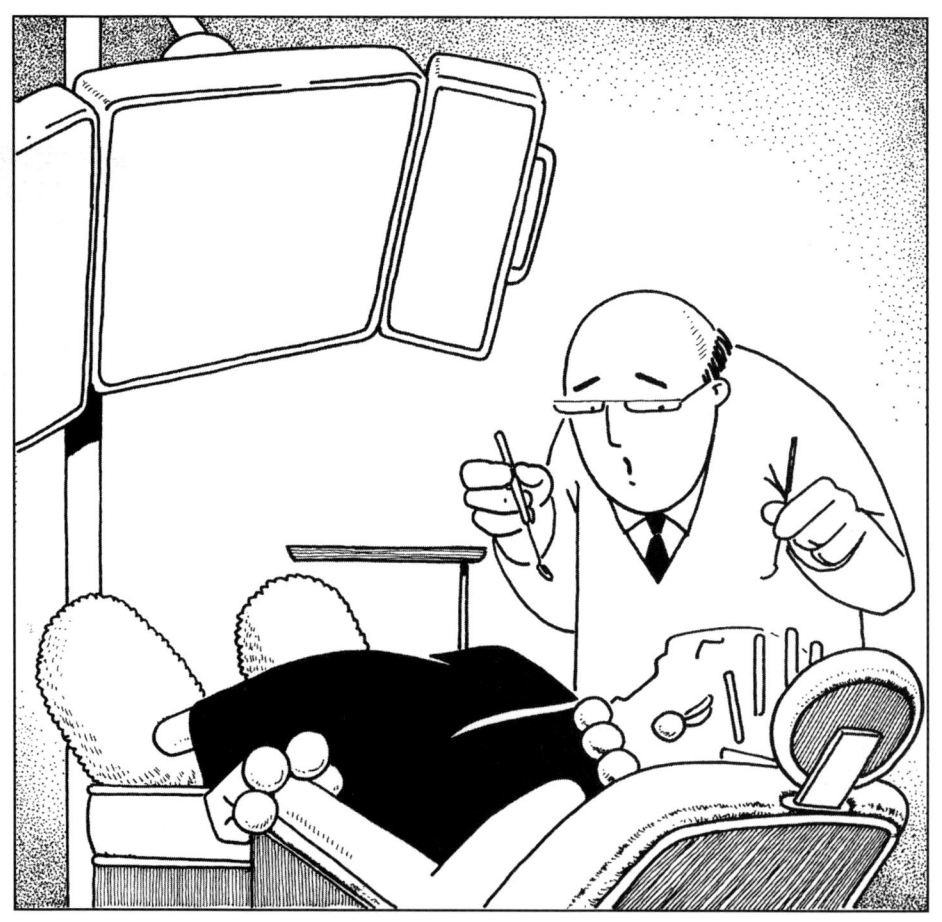

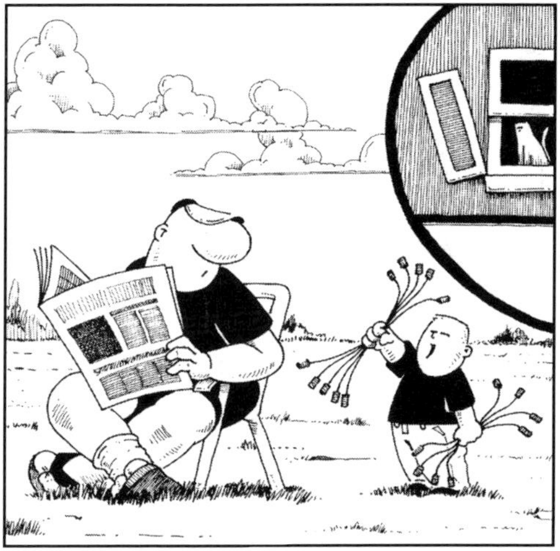

"Hey, Pop! Look at all these cool wires I found under the hood of the car!"

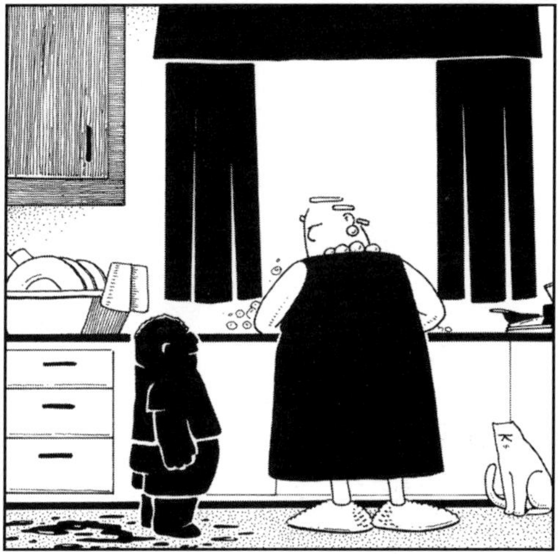

"Mom, our problems are solved. I struck oil underneath the car."

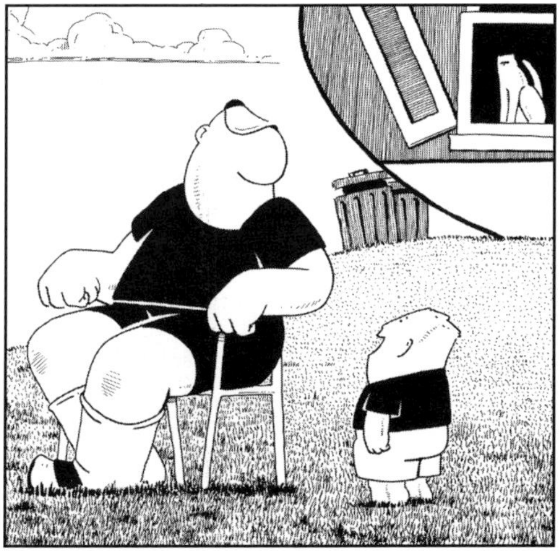

"Hey, Pop, when I get older, will you teach me how to drive the car while I'm asleep like Grandpa?"

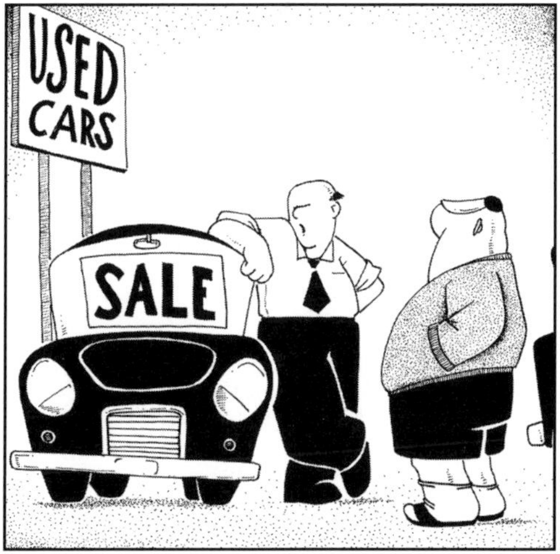
USED CARS
SALE

"This little gem has surprisingly low mileage, considering the previous owner lived in it for three years."

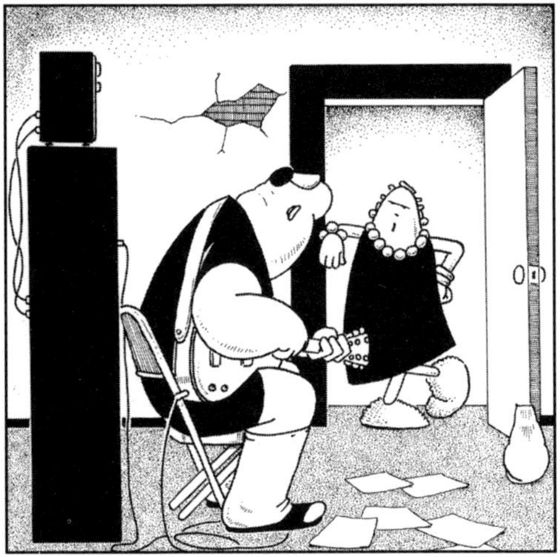

"I want to you sing at my funeral.
That way, everyone is sure to cry."

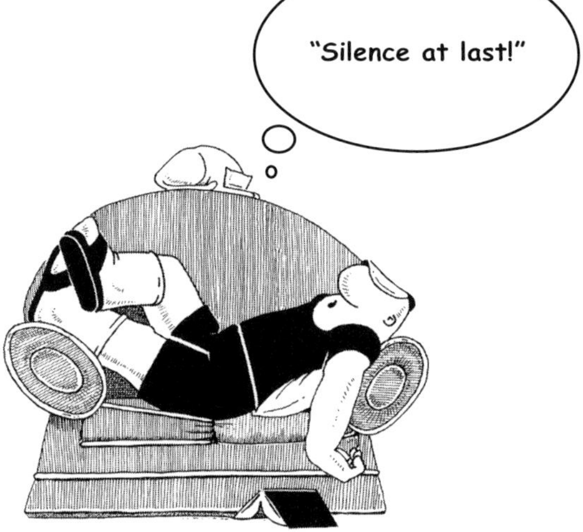
"Silence at last!"

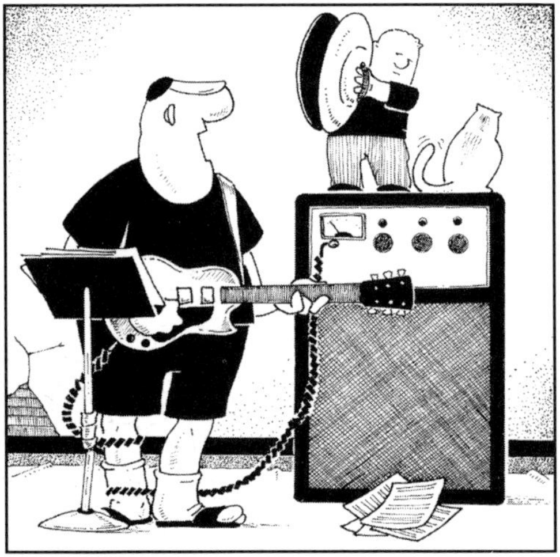

"That was pretty good. This time,
when I hit the augmented fifth,
step on the cat."

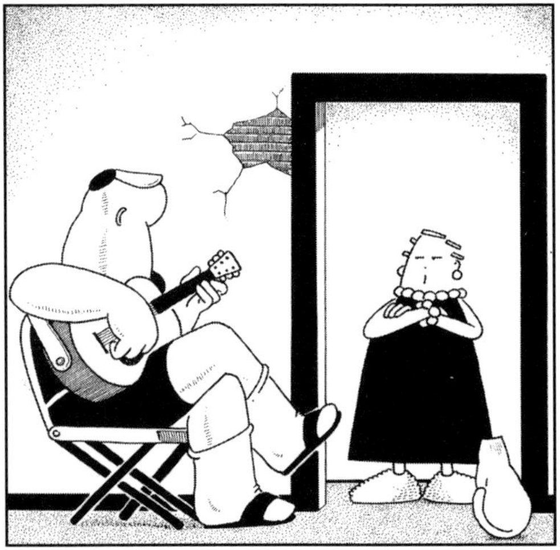

"I remember when you told me how badly
you wanted to play the guitar.
You've succeeded."

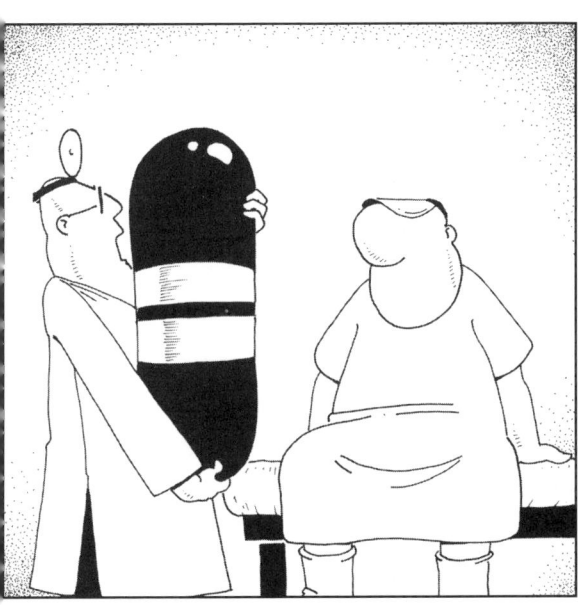

"Take this and call me if it doesn't kill you.""

"The kids are at your folks'. Whattaya say we dim the lights... open a bottle of wine... and watch pay-per-view wrestling?"

"Oh, I've seen this show. It's about a loving wife who suffers years of benign neglect and suddenly snaps and kills her husband. Everyone forgives her and she lives happily after."

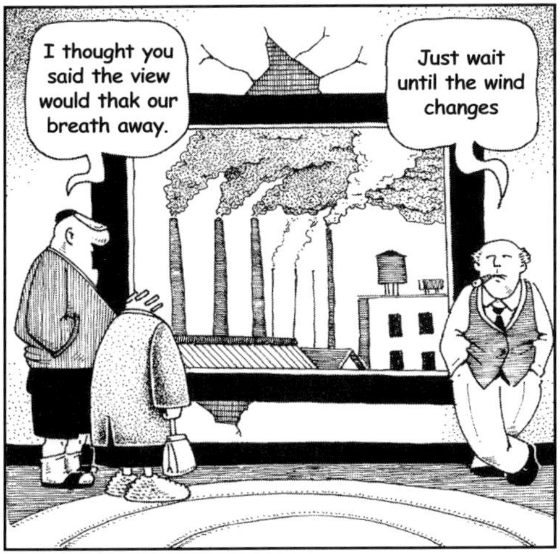
I thought you said the view would thak our breath away.
Just wait until the wind changes

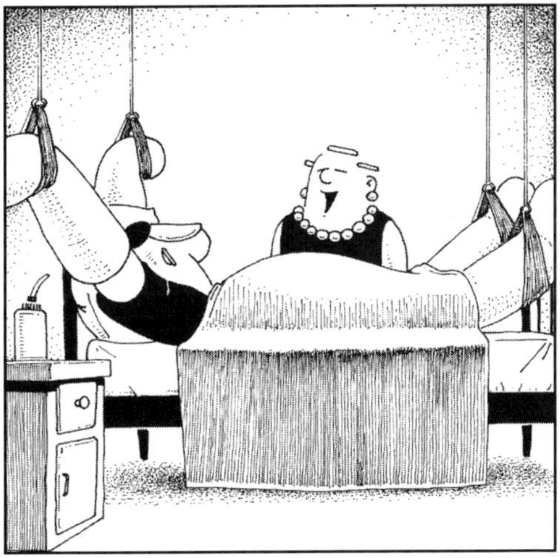

"Good news! The doctor said you had the cleanest underwear he'd ever seen!"

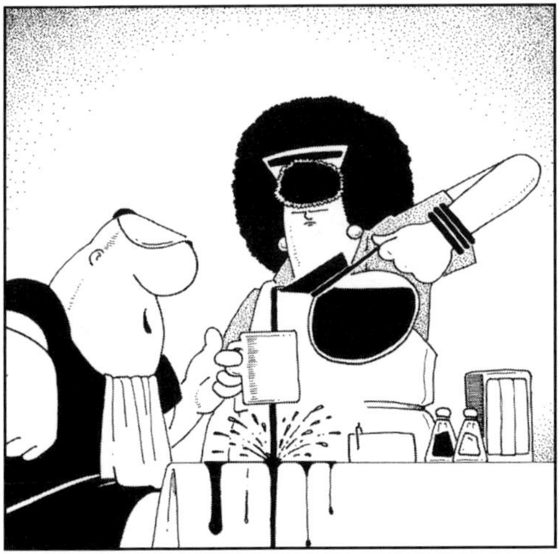

"Maggie, maybe a bottomless cup of coffee isn't such a great idea."

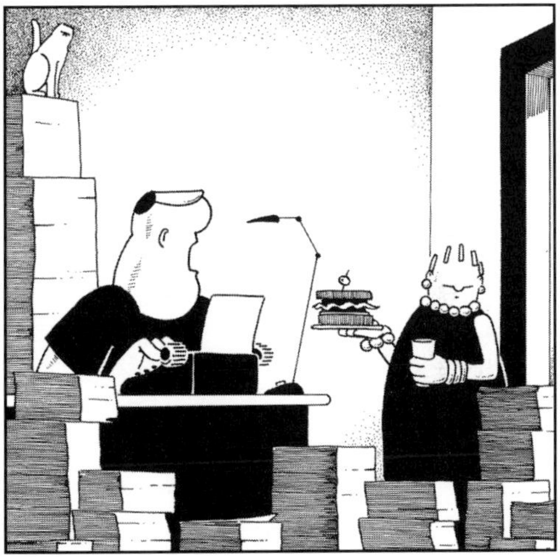

"Well, I finally finished my novel. Now, if I could just remember where I started..."

"Hello? Nine-One-One? Better come quick! I asked my wife if she wanted help with the laundry and she fainted dead-away."

"Well, you don't smell like P."

"We specialize in mergers."

"So... How was your vacation in the Amazon?"

"When you said the kids were at your mother's and we're going to have a ball, I thought... Ummhh... Never mind."

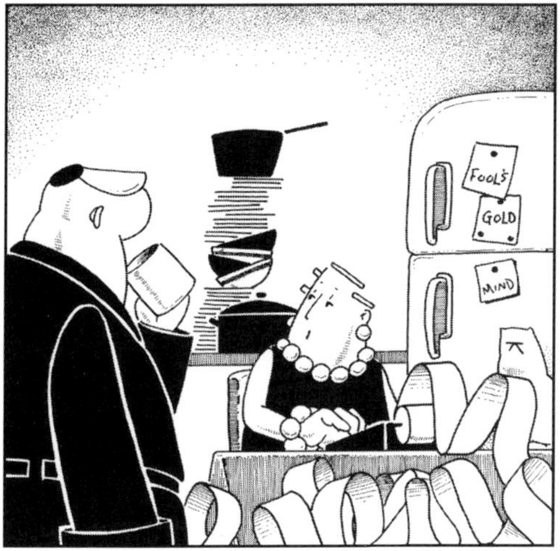
FOOL'S
GOLD
MIND

"I'd ask for your two cents,
but that's all the money we have left."

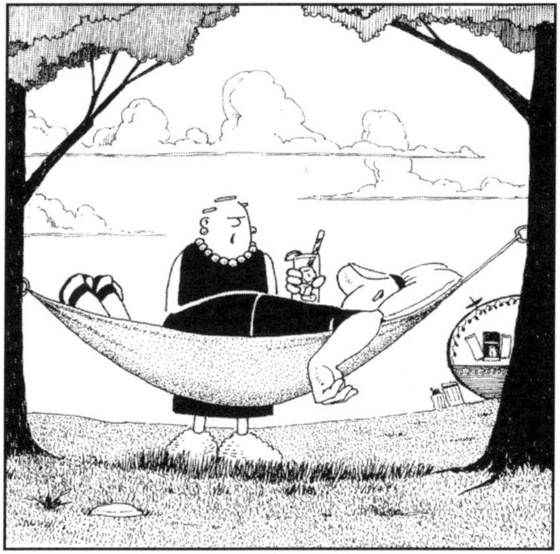

"American Idle called. You won.
Now, take down the Christmas lights."

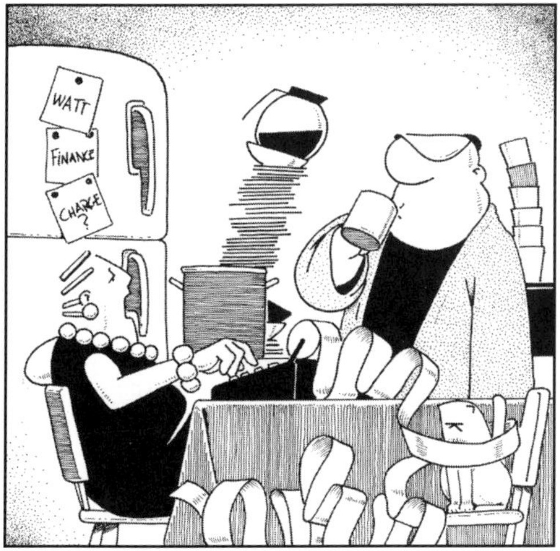
WATT
FINANCE
CHANGE
?

"Let me put it this way. As soon as they
shut off the electricity, we'll be
in the black."

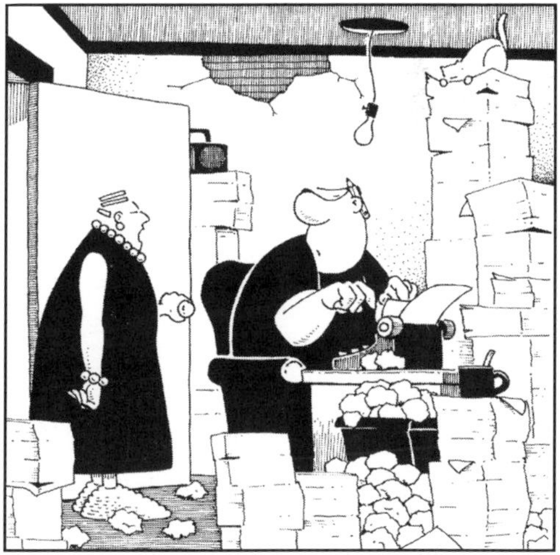

"I'm afraid I have bad news.
The great American novel has
already been written."

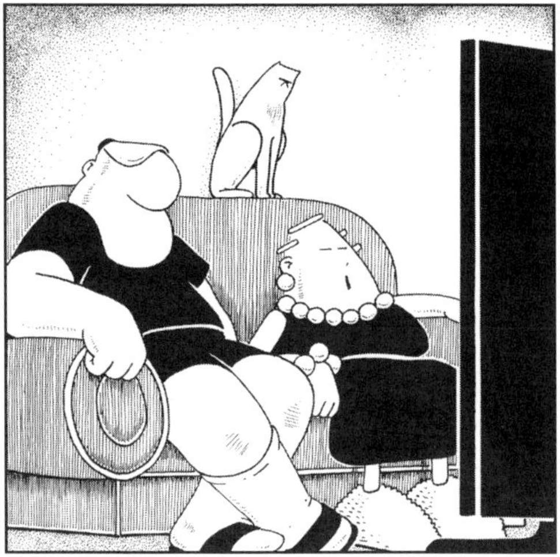

"I feel a chuckle coming on.
Switch to the news."

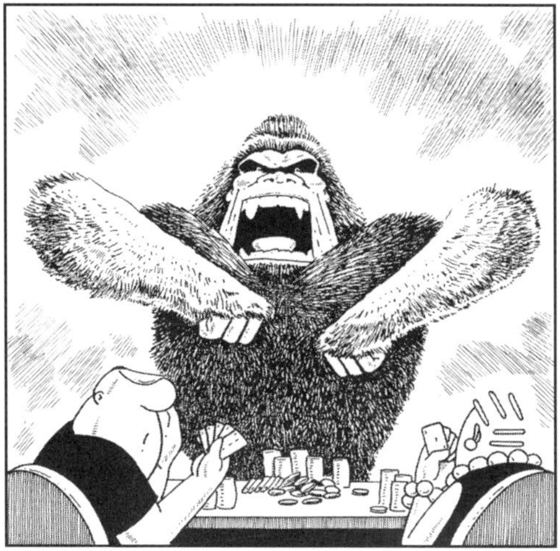

"It's a bluff. I saw it on Discovery."

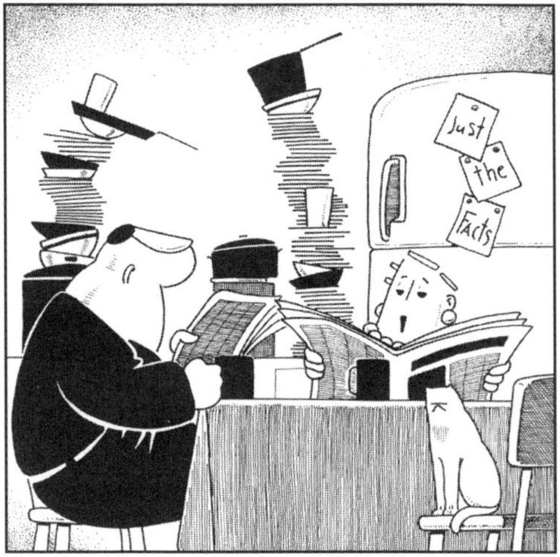
Just
the
Facts

"It says here, Americans' attention
spans are getting shorter every...
Oh, look! Coupons!"

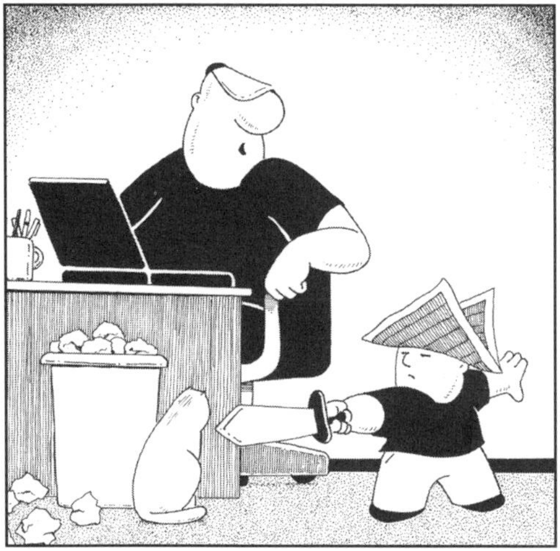

"How about showing me how
to hack through this parental
guard software again."

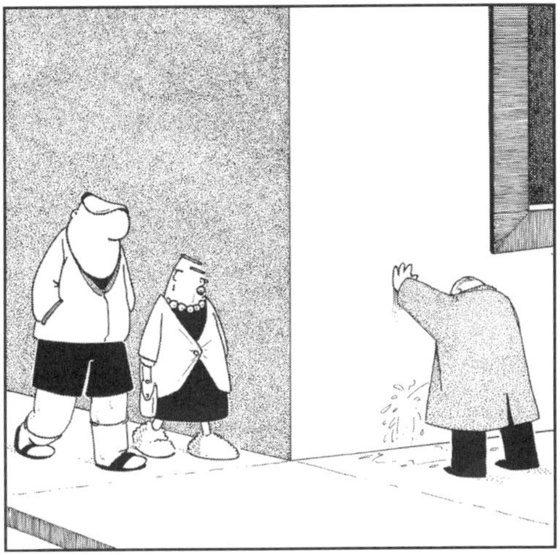

"Oh, quit whining!
Good times are just around the corner!"

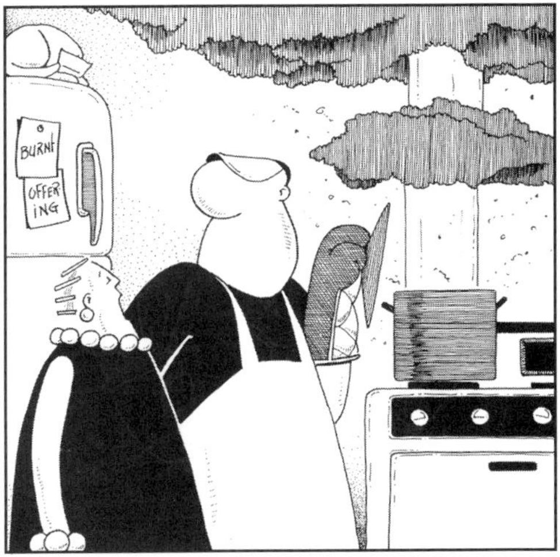
BURNT
OFFERING

"You say it's chili, but I say
it's a recipe for disaster."

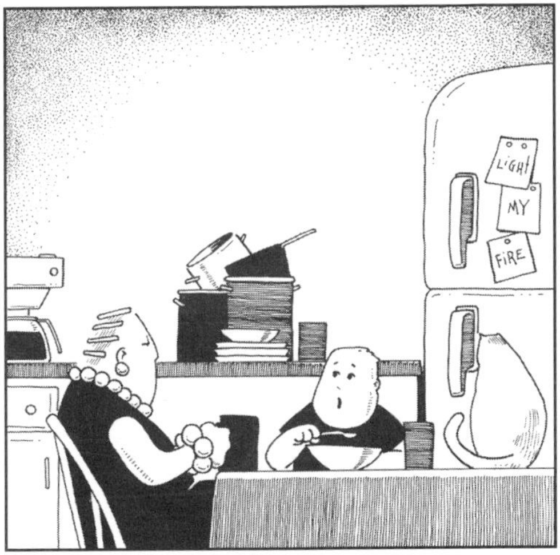
LIGHT
MY
FIRE

"If Gramma wouldn't let Dad
play with matches, how did he
learn to light a fart?"

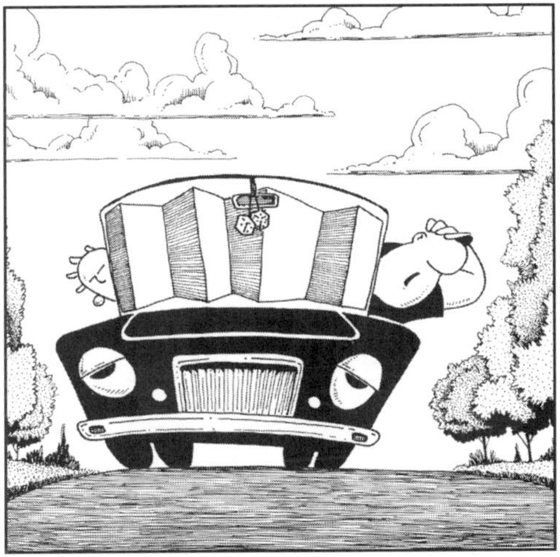

"These windshield screens are great
at blocking the heat, but they sure
make it tough to see."

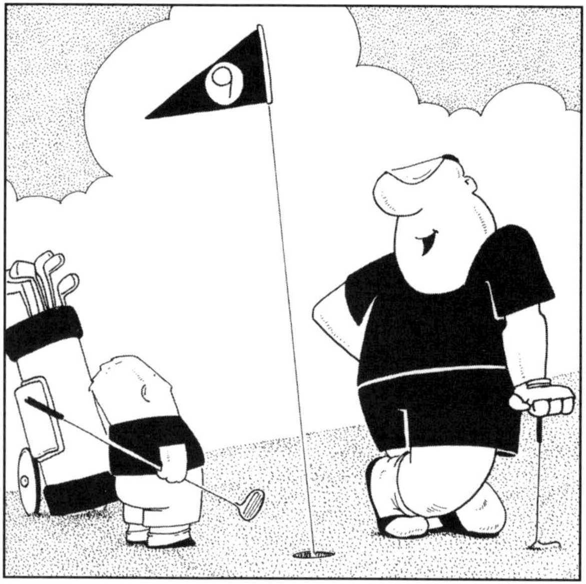
9

"Well... I finally broke a hundred! Whattaya say we play the back nine?"

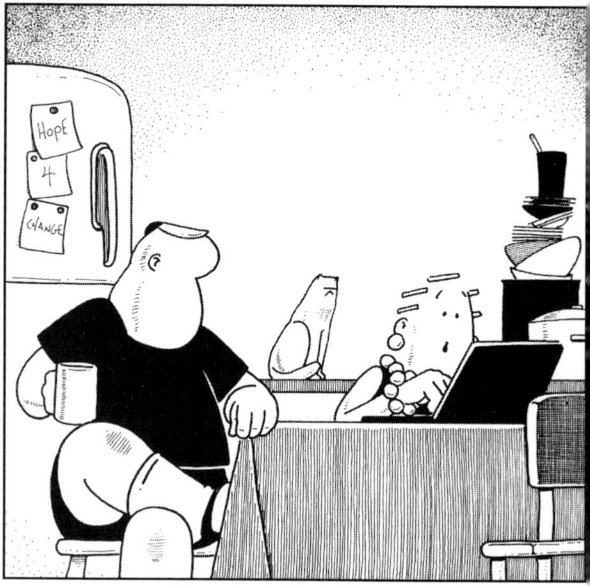
HOPE
4
CHANGE

"Just now... I balanced the checkbook and hit 'reconcile'... and I thought I heard a scream."

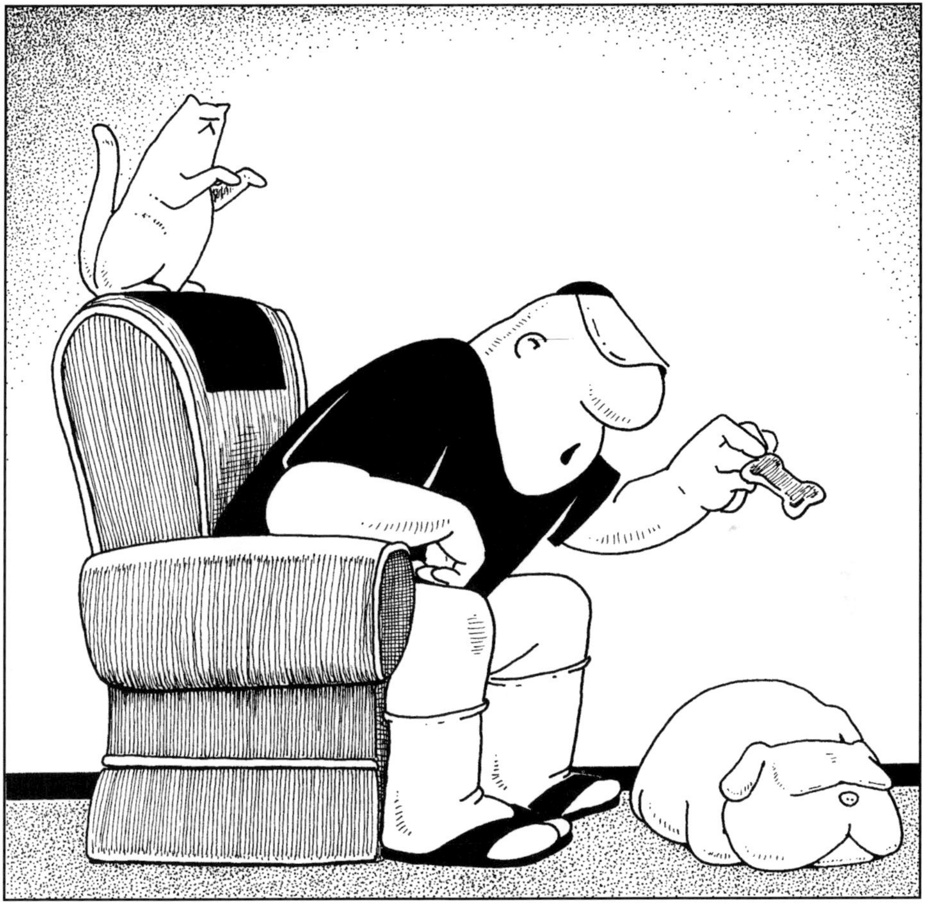

"C'mon, boy... Sit up! Beg! I said, BEG!
Stupid dog..."

"What do you mean 'Blu-ray is better than real life'? ANYTHING is better than real life!"

"We've got a 60" TV, over two hundred channels all in high definition, Showtime, HBO, Tivo, Playstation and Netflix... and you're bored?"

"The remote's working fine. You're staring at the window."

"At last! Something intelligent on the TV."

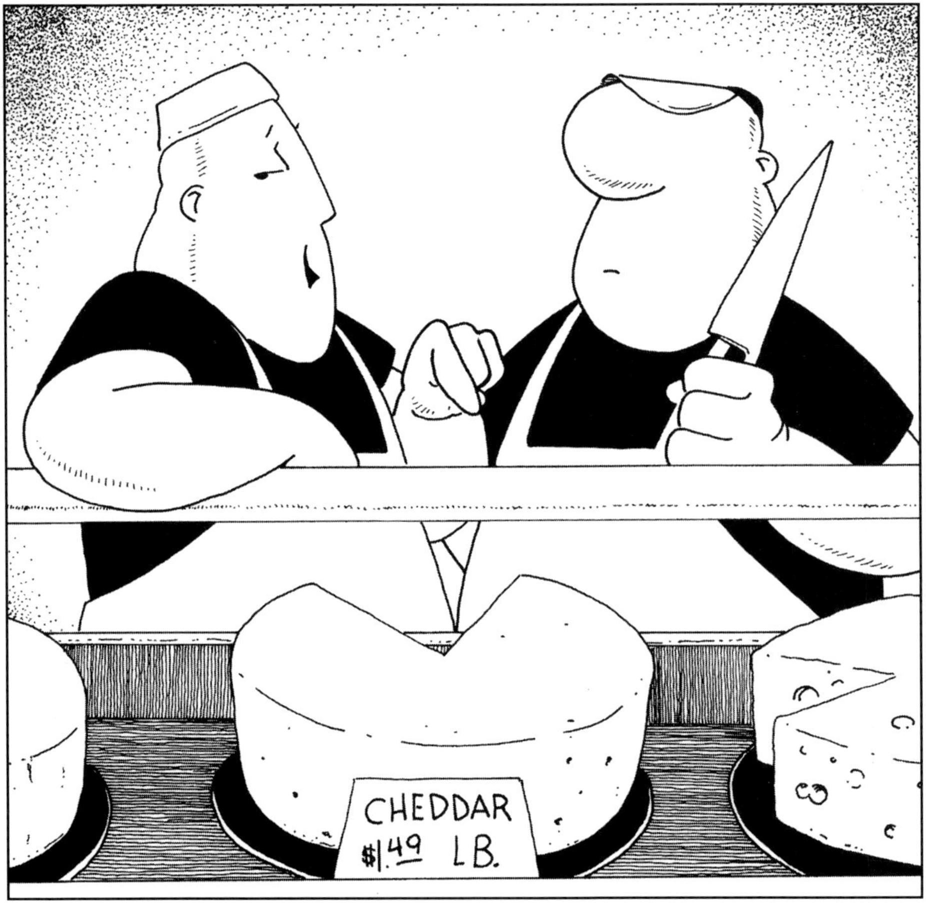
CHEDDAR
$1.49 LB.

"Perhaps I wasn't clear in the job description. You're supposed to cut THIS cheese."

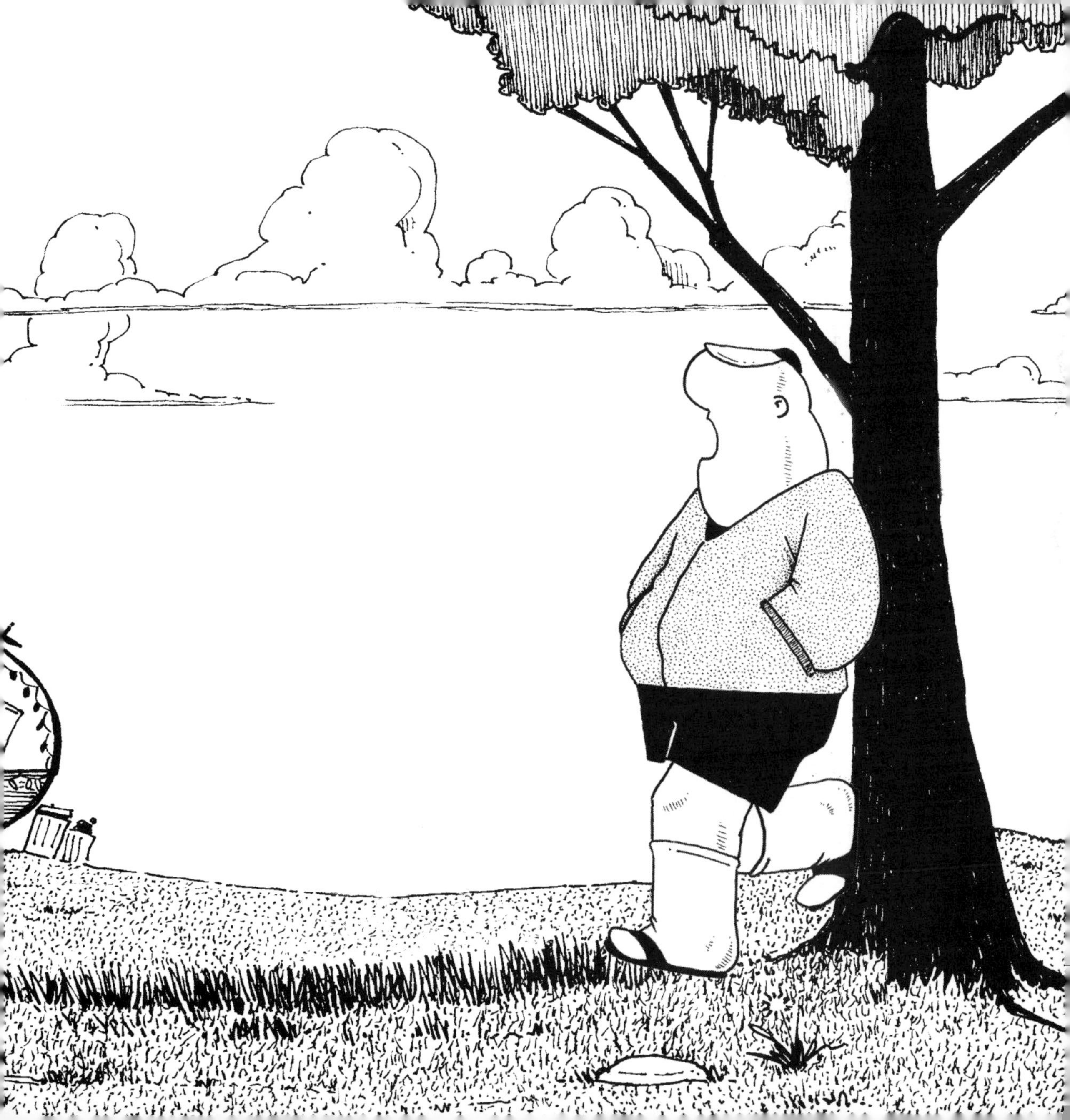

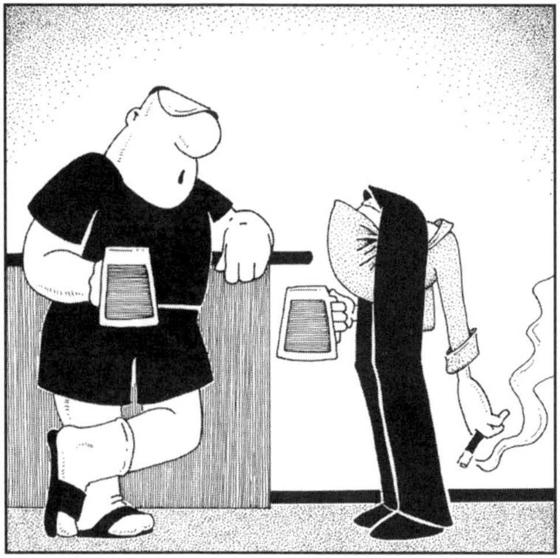

"Let me guess... You're in politics."

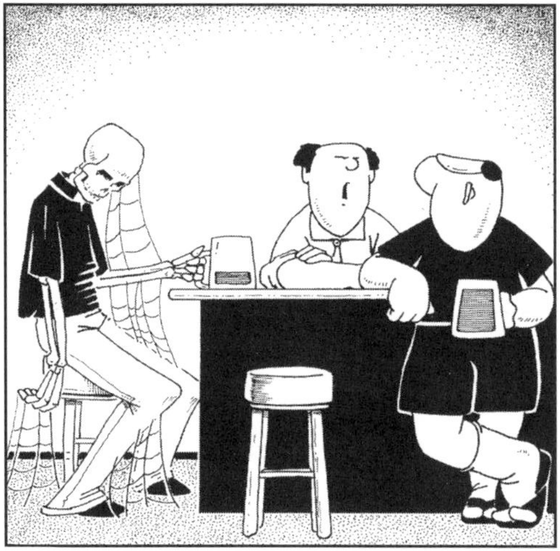

"It's been slow."

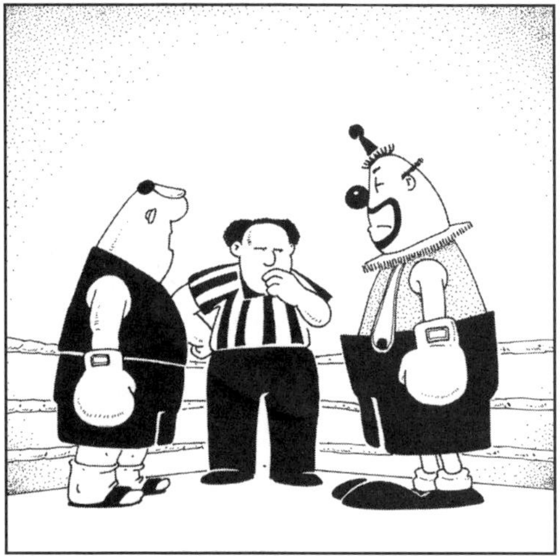

"I thought you said no funny stuff."

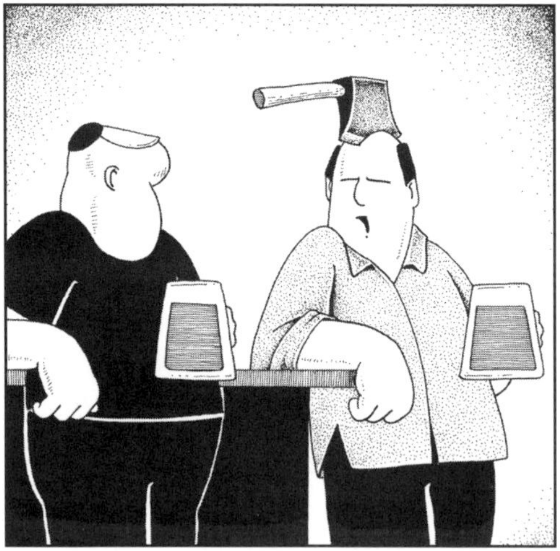

"'Kiss and make up,' she said...
'Bury the hatchet,' she said."

"For God's sake, Bud! First you lose an arm and a leg at keno and now THIS!"

"Sweetheart, I'm so proud of you. You've made a complete fool of yourself."

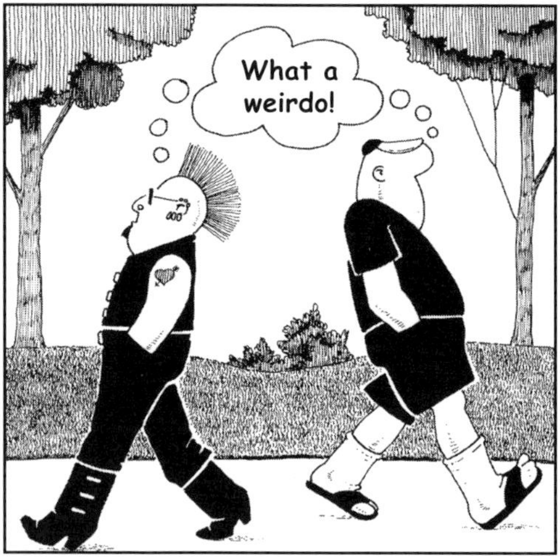
What a weirdo!

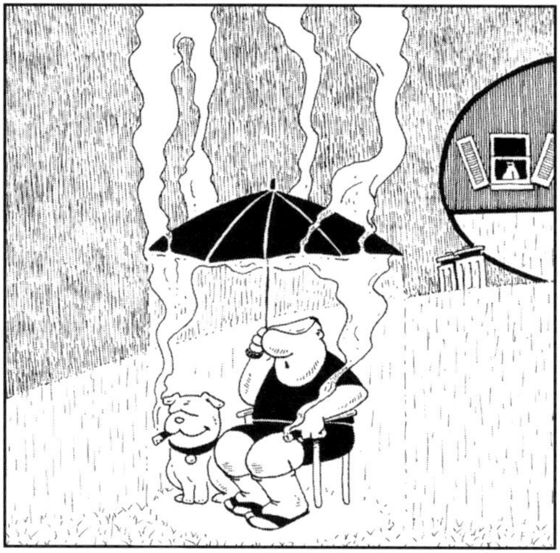

"The problem with that woman is she just doesn't appreciate a good cigar."

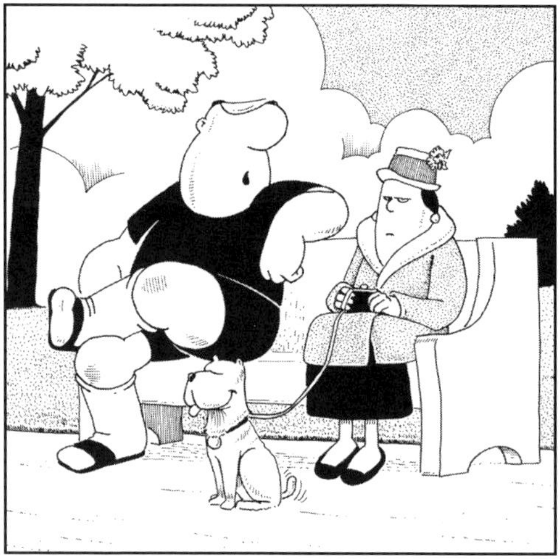

"Your dog looks happy. I thought they were supposed to resemble their owners."

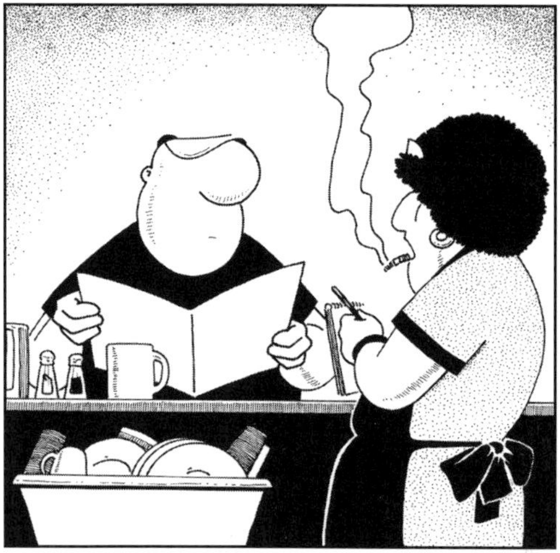

"We don't take Visa, Master Card, Discover, American Express or bovine excrement. Now... What can I get you?"

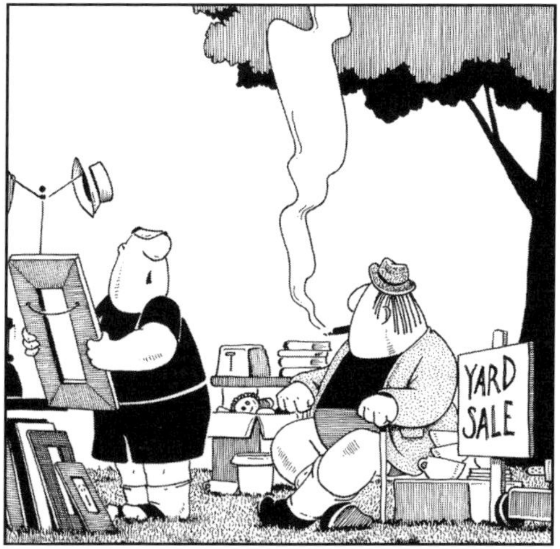
YARD SALE

"Nice picture!
I'll give you a thousand words for it."

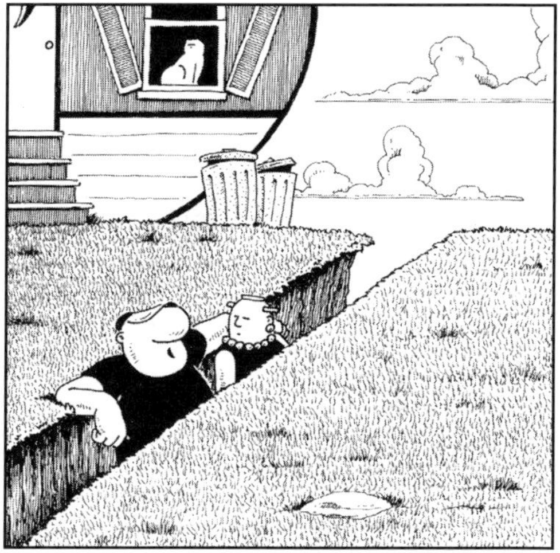

"I think you're right, sweetheart.
We ARE in a rut."

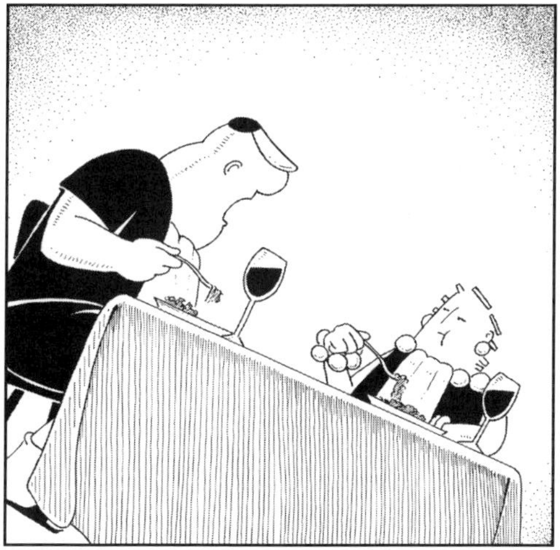

"Is it me, or is
this place going downhill?"

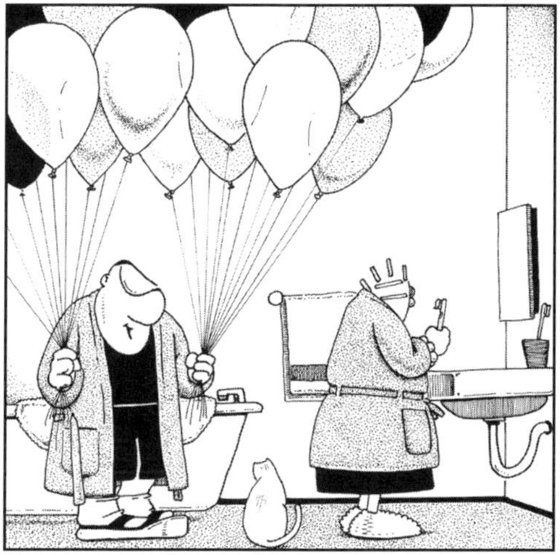

"HAH! I told you I could lose
five pounds in twenty four hours!"

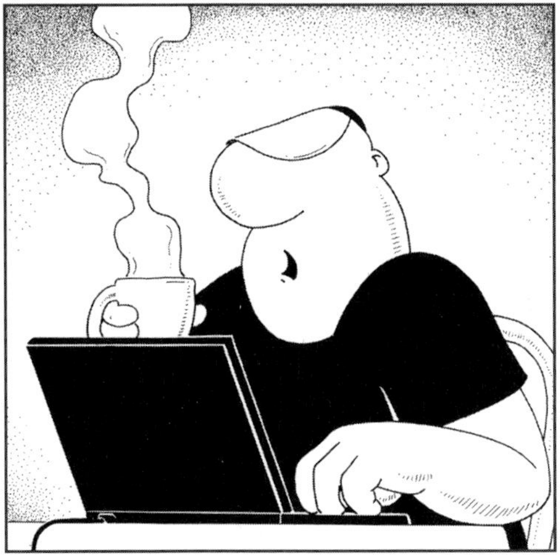

"Dude! You're on Skype! Wear pants!"

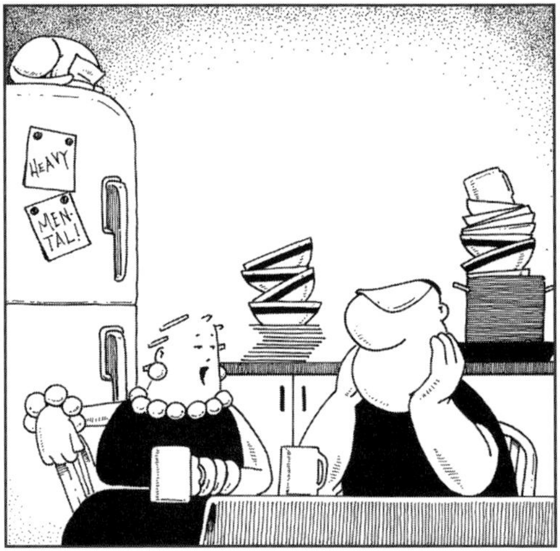
HEAVY
MEN-TAL!

"Assuming you haven't lost it again,
what's on your mind?"

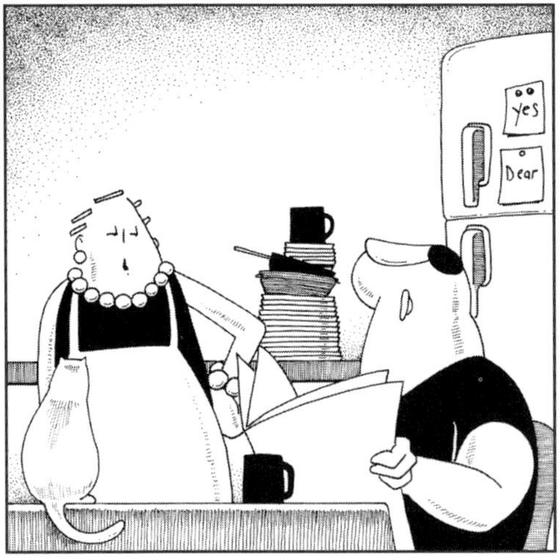
yes
Dear

"Dear, let's agree to compromise
and do it my way."

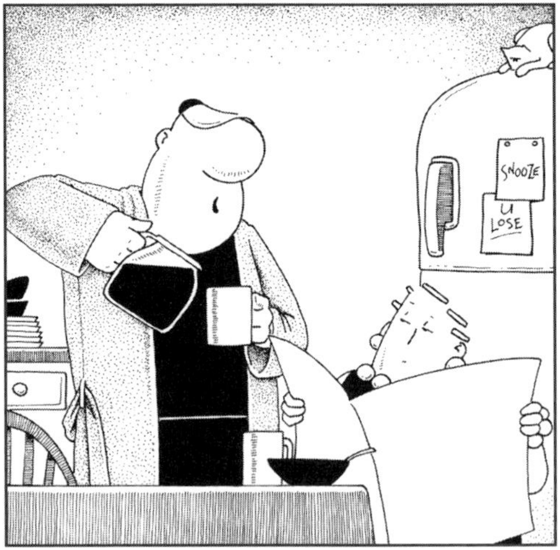
SNOOZE
U LOSE

"Well, I'm up.
What are your other two wishes?"

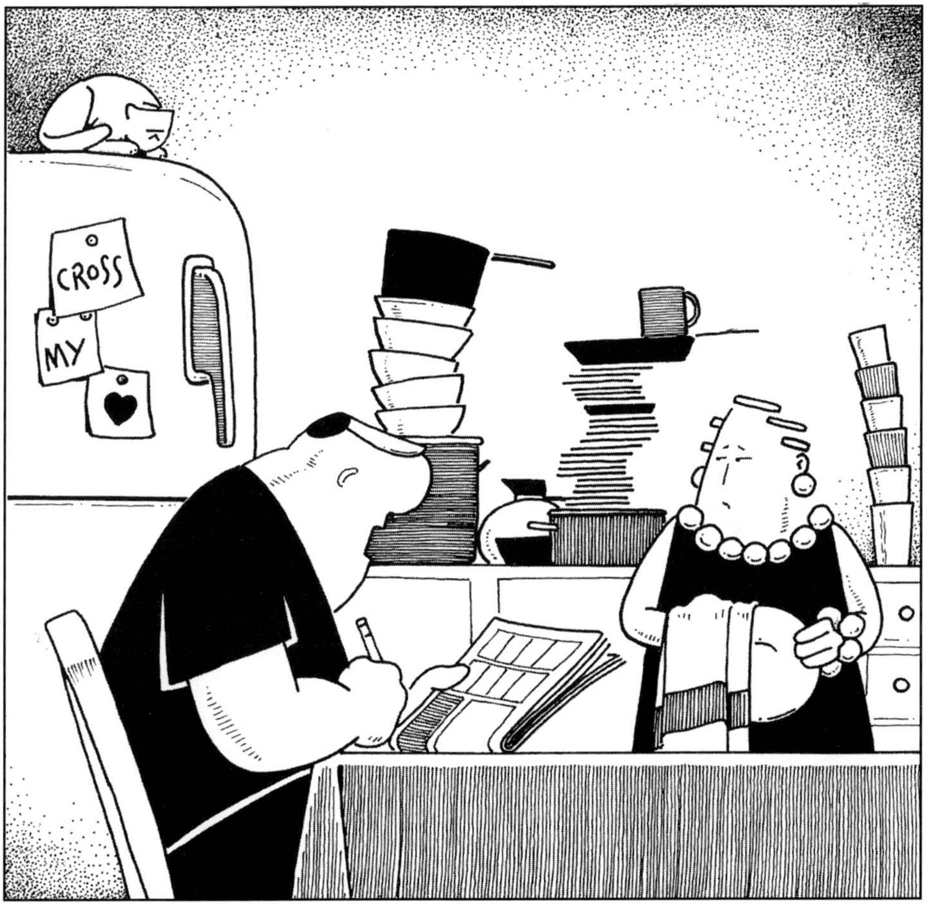
CROSS
MY

"Seven letters. The clue is 'shiftless loser.' Starts with 'H.' Ends with 'D.' "

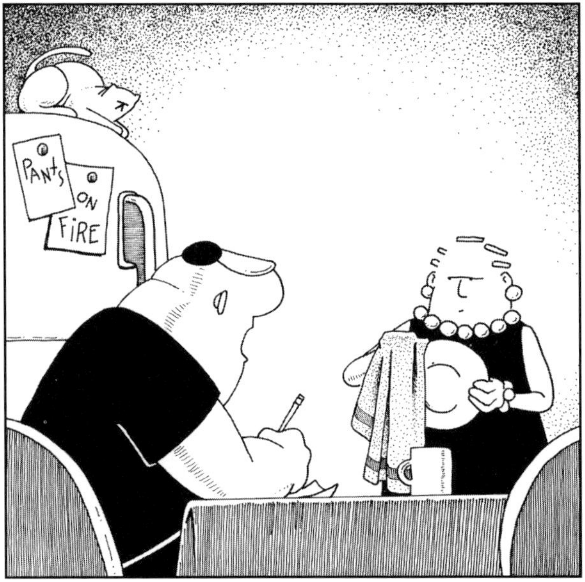
PANTS ON FIRE

"Oh, come on, dear, everyone fudges on their resume. Now... How do you spell Mensa?"

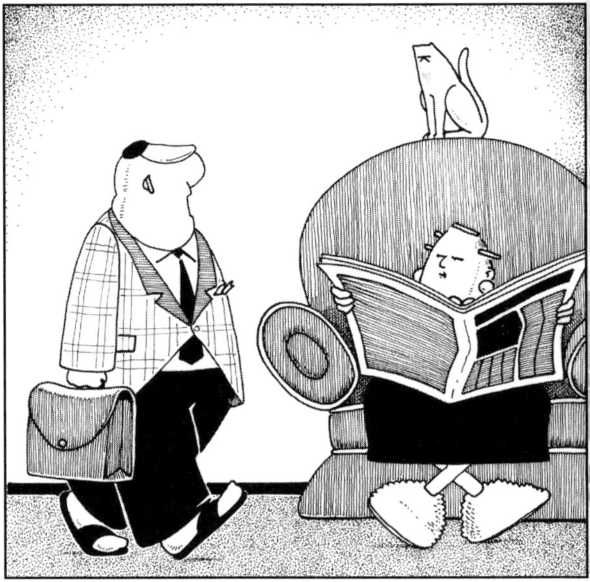

"The lady at the employment office said my sports coat is a real faux pas. Is that some fancy french designer?"

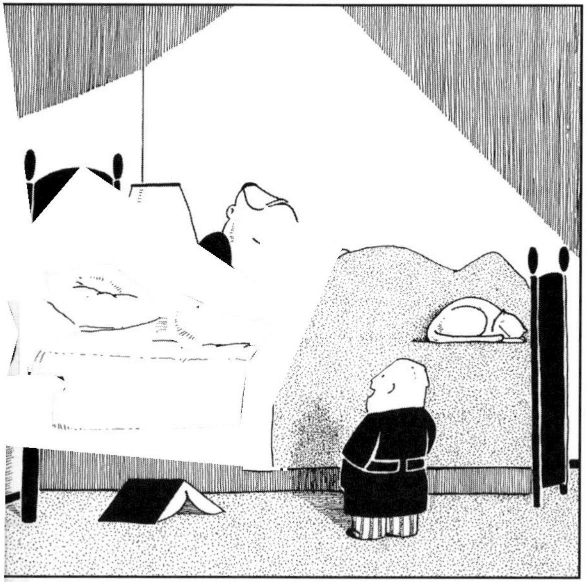

"Pop, I can't sleep. How about telling me another tragic yarn from your hard-scrabble youth? That always knocks me out like Nyquil."

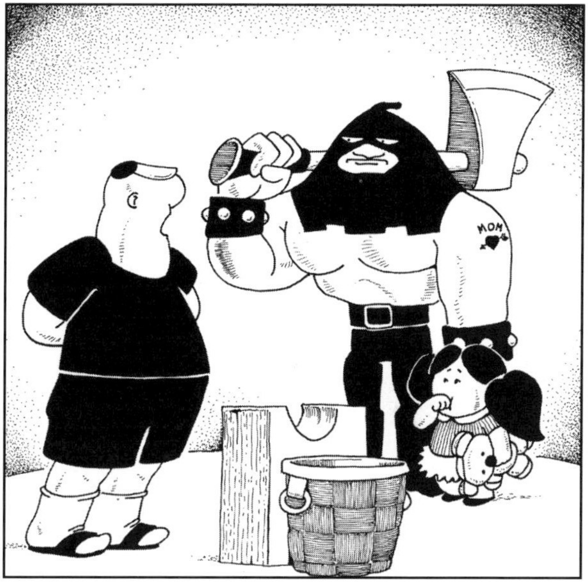
MOM

"Dude! Really!!
'Take Your Daughter to Work' day?!!"

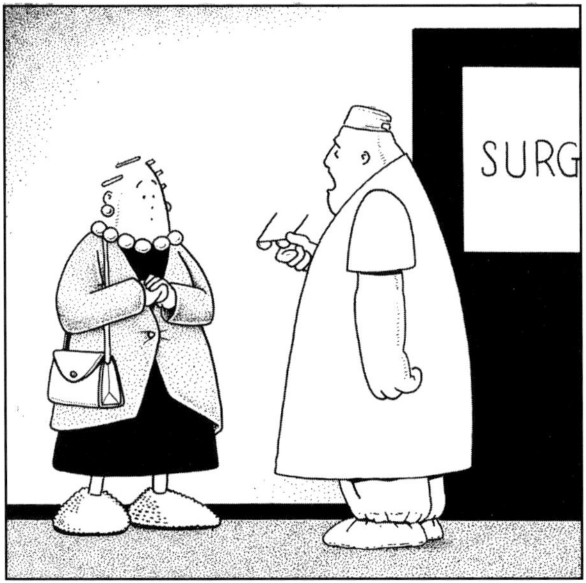
SURG

"We did everything we could,
but he pulled through anyway."

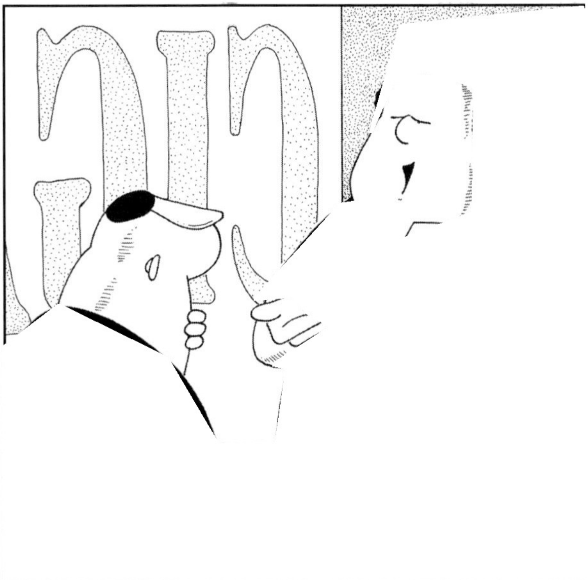

"These are a robust blend of long-leaf Dominican
tobaccos, fortified with extra testosterone."

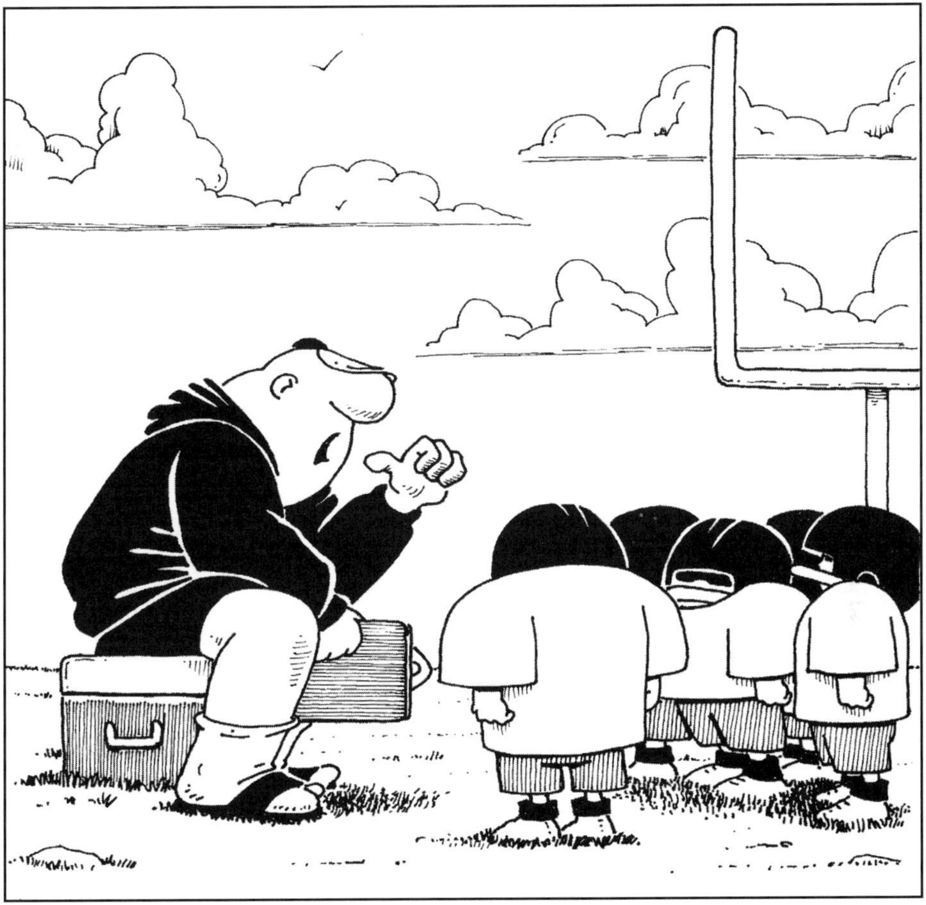

"So... Go out there and make old coach proud, or he's going to have to have another drink."

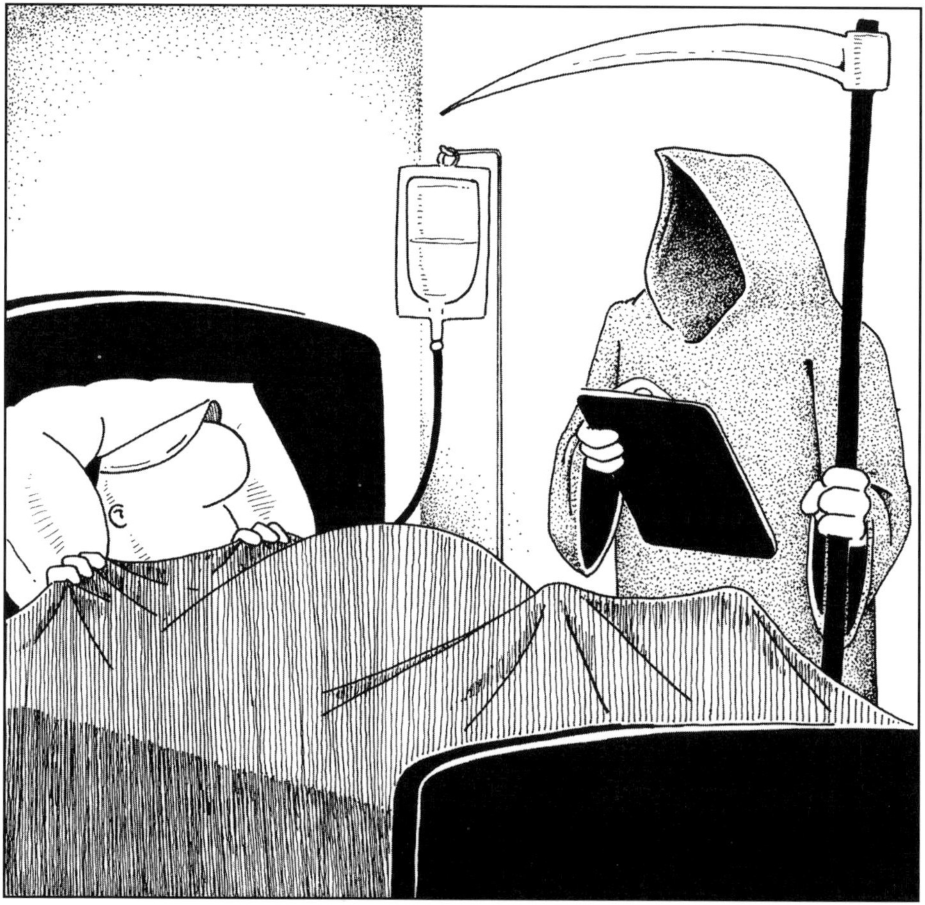

"Relax, I'm the doctor. It's Halloween."

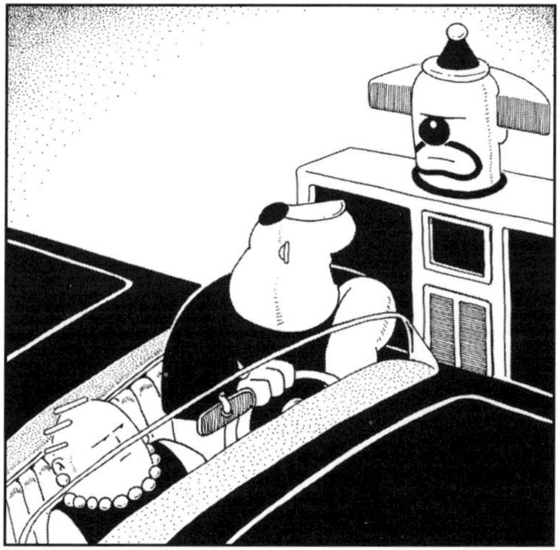

"Oh! Put a candle on that veggie burger. It's my wife's birthday."

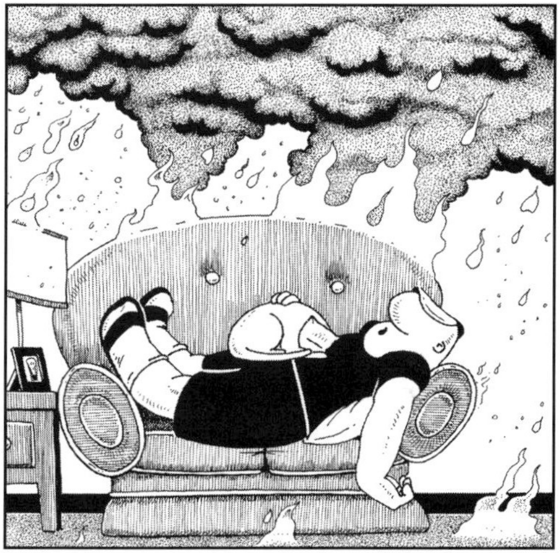

"Kitty, I think I'm going to HAVE to get up."

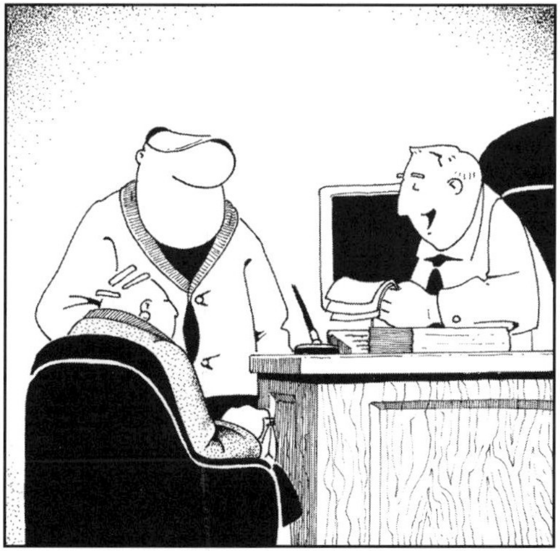

"After reviewing your application for our low-interest loan, I'm relieved to say we have no interest whatsoever."

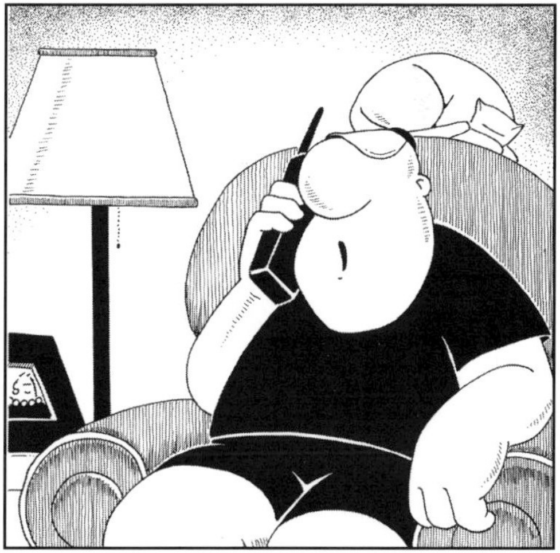

"Thanks for asking. I intend to vote for the candidate who doesn't call me on the phone."

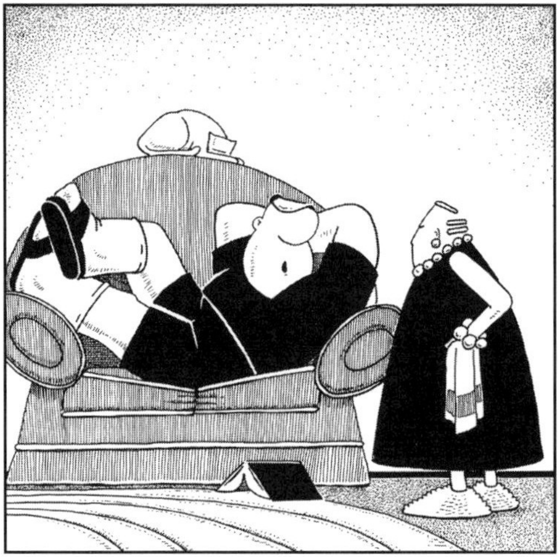

"I am ignoring you, Dear,
but I'm doing it with love."

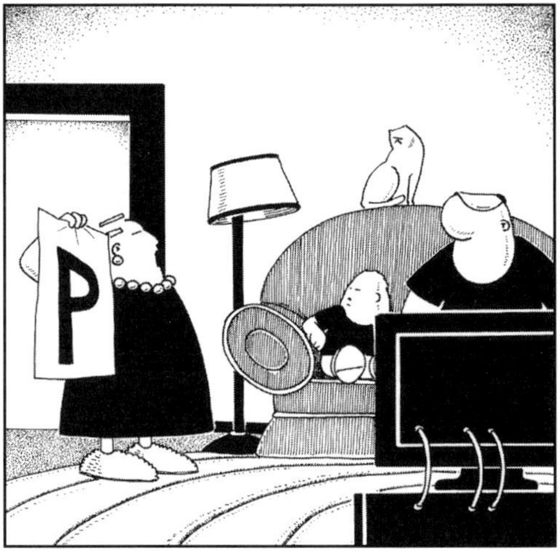
P

"Which one of you gentlemen left this
on the bathroom floor?"

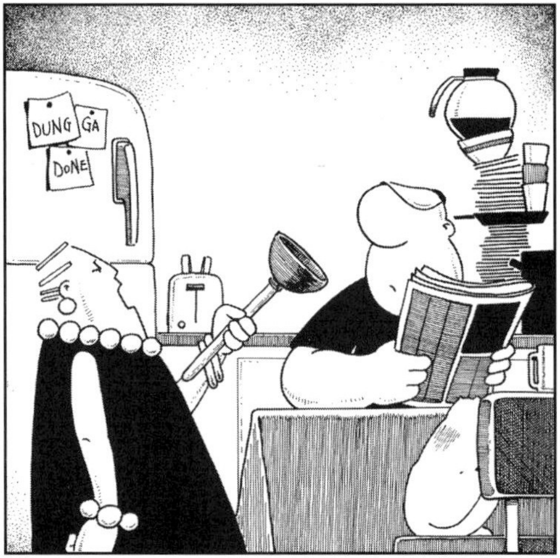
DUNG
GA
DONE

"Stardate - March first. The Captain's
log has clogged the toilet again."

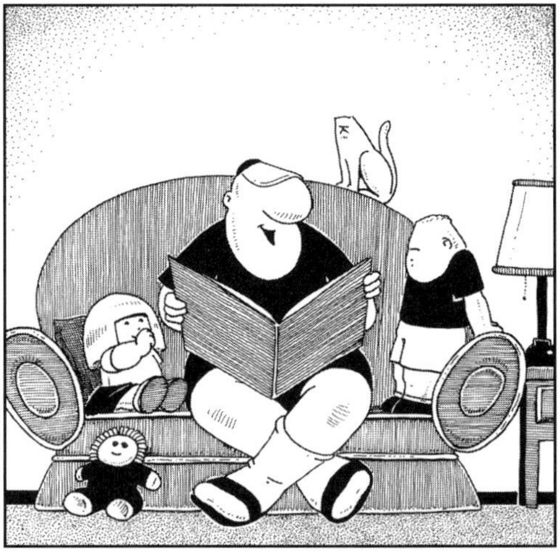

"...And the children made their loving
father a delicious snack and
they all lived happily ever after."

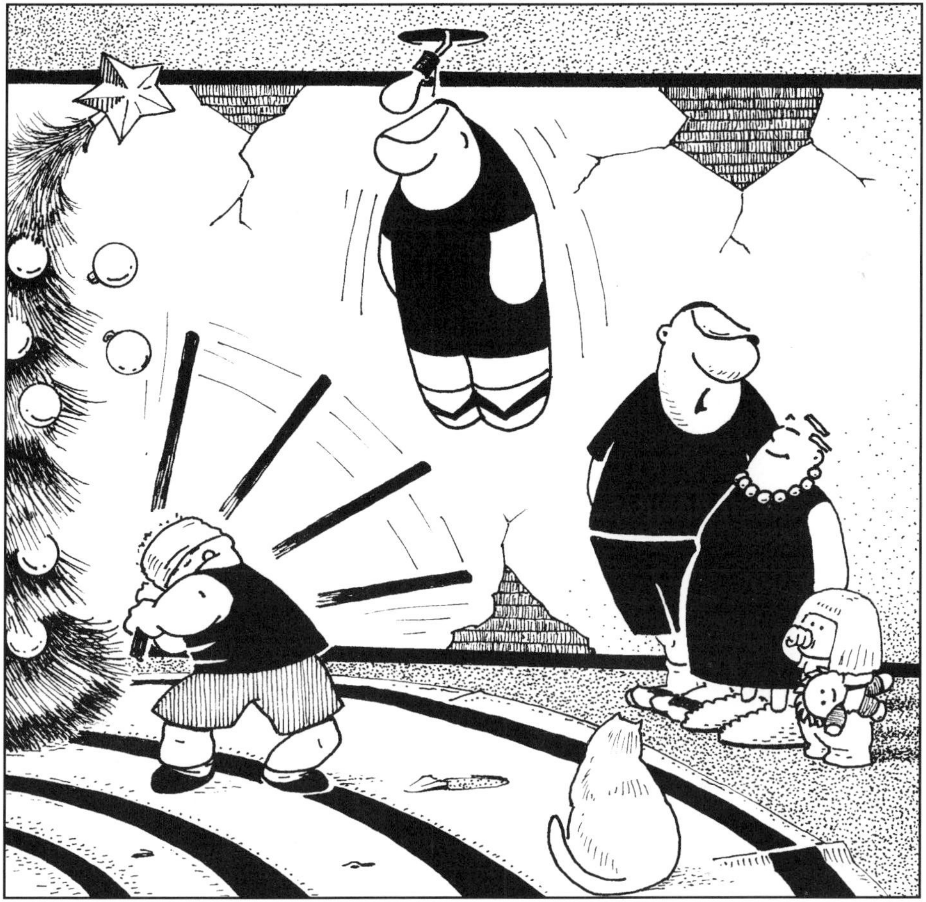

"Let me guess...
Your mother picked out the piñata."

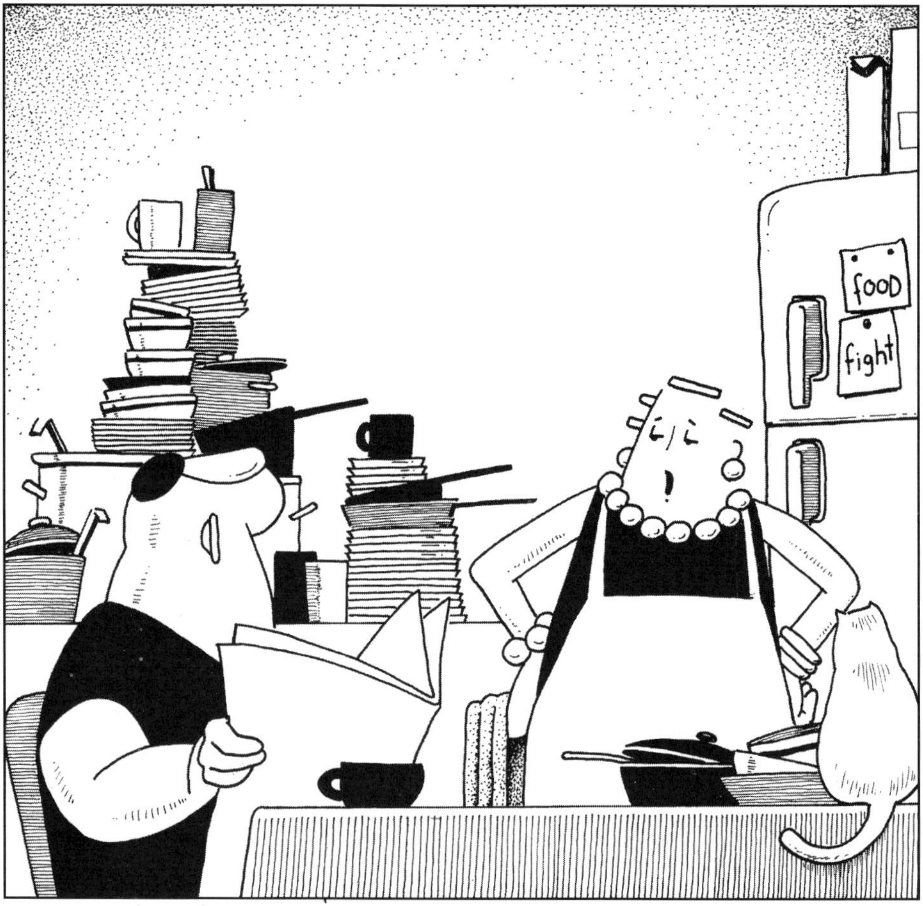
food
fight

"I don't feel like doing the dishes.
Say something stupid so I can throw them at you."

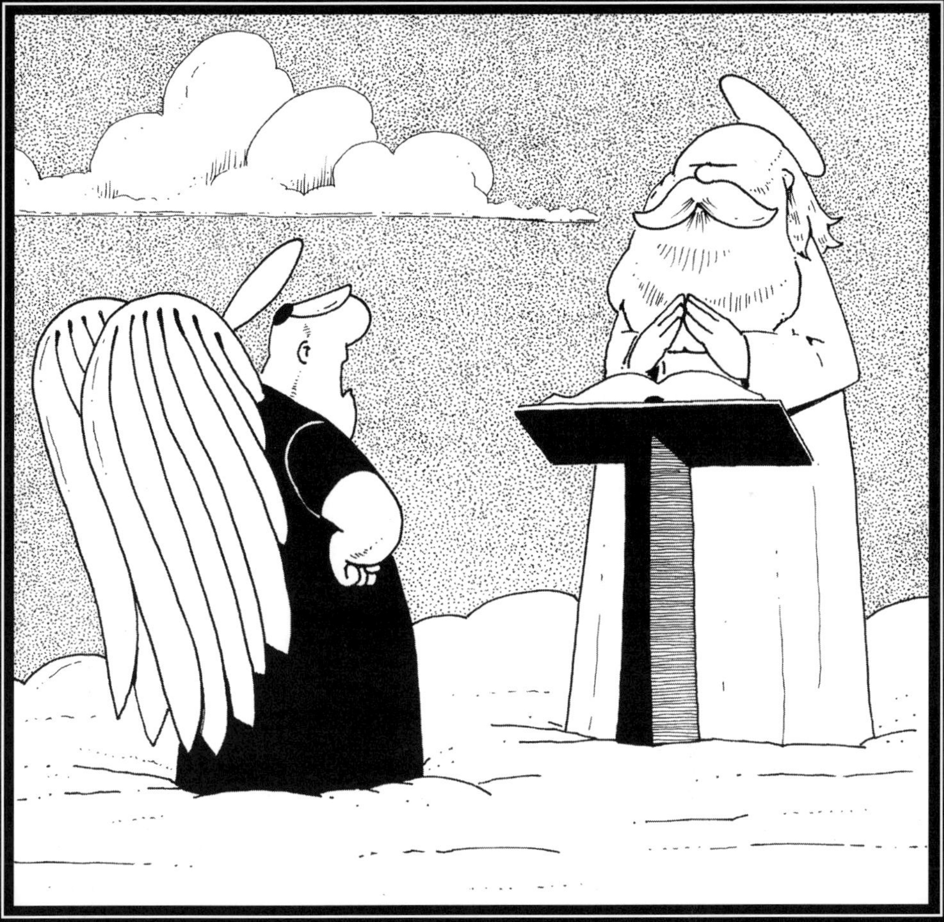

"Give me a break! The 'Hokey Pokey?!!' THAT's what it's all about?!!"

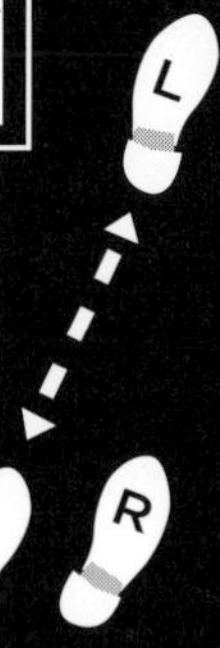
L
R
L

Brad's first cartoons appeared in 1992 and ran continuously until 2000 when he left the newspaper business to pursue a career as a freelance illustrator

His comics have appeared in *Funny Times*, the *Cleveland Plain Dealer*, the *Charleston Daily Mail* (Charleston, WV), the now-defunct *Nashville Banner*, and the *Reno Gazette Journal*, as well as various other smaller paper too numerous to mention.

Besides illustration, Brad has also been a bartender, baker, carpet layer, writer and ambitiously irresponsible. He's also very good at expressing opinions on things he knows nothing about.

Currently, Brad lives in reno, Nevada with his wife and their cat.